the Parable of the
Two Souls
the hidden foundation
of Christianity

B. Lee McDowell

B. Lee McDowell

The Parable of the Two Souls

Published by Dowadad Press
    A division of Lee McDowell Christian Ministries, Inc.
    Nacogdoches, TX
    www.blmcm.net

ISBN # 978-0-9980359-8-7

All Scripture quotations are taken from the King James Version of the Bible.

Printed in the United States of America.

Dedication

This book is dedicated to everyone, in the hopes
that all may come to know a hidden mystery
of Spiritual Truth long unknown by many.
That could involve a sinner becoming a Saint.
That could involve a Saint becoming aware
they have two souls which opens
a new understanding of who they are,
think like they do, and sometimes act in confusing ways.

This book provides the solution for any Saint
to Live in freedom and Truth.

Acknowledgements

God
for creating His Spiritual Life in me

Jesus Christ
my Savior, my Friend

Holy Spirit
my Teacher of Spiritual Truth

Contents

The Parable of the Two Souls

Foreword

Hello friends in Christ!

You are in store for a great awakening of Holy Scriptural Truth. I pray you are a Spiritually born again Christian. And if you are, have you ever wondered why you still "mess up" sometimes? We say things we shouldn't, do things we shouldn't, and think many things we shouldn't. Why after receiving the Holy Spirit at our new Spiritual birth do we continue to sin?

Lee's book *The Images of God and Man* completely answered that question for me. This book, *The Parable of the Two Souls,* gives me more understanding and appreciation for who every Christian is Spiritually. Wow! What an awakening for me and it can now be for you. While we have received through the Holy Spirit, the Mind, Emotions, and Will of God, we still possess the residue of the old natural sinful spiritual mind, emotions, and will we were physically born with.

The apostle Paul clearly outlines our dilemma in Romans 7:14-17 (Struggling with sin, NLT). "So the trouble is not with the law, for it is spiritual and good. The trouble is with me, for I am all too human, a slave to sin. I don't really understand myself, for I want to do what is right, but I don't do it. Instead, I do what I hate. But if I know that what I am doing is wrong, this shows that I agree that the law is good. So I am not the one doing wrong; it is the sin living in me that does it."

Now you and I can understand the Truth of what we are dealing with. Two minds, two sets of emotions, and two wills (decision makers). One each in the Two Souls. The Truth will empower you to focus on God's Mind, Emotions, and Will that you received when you were Spiritually born again. Read on friends!

David Ruby

Preface

This book is about spiritual things. Physical things are not part of the spiritual realm, even though the spiritual does impact the physical in many ways. Every individual is a physical AND spiritual being. And what is known as being Born Again/New Creation, the spiritual changes are dramatical. All of these are easily seen with the diagrams included in this book.

The vast majority of my writing today is about post-Pentecost Truth. It was first at Pentecost that Saints were given Holy Spirit to indwell their earthsuits. This changed every Saint's Spiritual Life in a big way.

With Holy Spirit indwelling, the trichotomy of a Saint becomes a very interesting picture. No longer an earth being without the capacity to have a very intimate personal relationship and fellowship with Holy God.

The history of becoming a Saint is important to understand what, where, and when the two souls come into being. We will look into the difference between being a sinner and a Saint.

This will be a journey. It will be for someone who desires to get out of the dry land of the wilderness of trying to live the Christian life, and get into and live in the promised land filled with Holy Spirit. Do not get weary before the *fruit* (Life) is gleaned from all the Truth presented here. Just like for a gardener, farmer, or husbandman of the vineyard, there is some work to be done before the harvest of the ultimate Life is enjoyed. It will be more than sweet when you taste of the *fruit* of *The Parable of the Two Souls*.

B. Lee McDowell

chapter 1

Revelation

Now to him that is of power to stablish you
according to my gospel, and the preaching of Jesus Christ,
according to the revelation of the mystery,
which was kept secret since the world began,
But now is made manifest,
and by the scriptures of the prophets,
according to the commandment of the everlasting God,
made known to all nations for the obedience of faith:
To God only wise, be glory through Jesus Christ for ever.
Romans 16:25-27

Here is God's secret of knowing, understanding, believing, and receiving His Truth. *Revelation.* Without revelation from God there is no knowledge of Spiritual Truth which renders understanding, believing, and receiving Truth an impossible venture.

Numerous times in Scripture God has revealed the importance of His revelation. So let us take a look at several of these verses to set the stage for Seeing the hidden mystery of the Two souls. (these are presented in chronological order as they appear in the New Testament with a mixture of *reveal, revealed,* and *revelation)*

> At that time Jesus answered and said, I thank thee, O Father, Lord of heaven and earth, because thou hast hid these things from the wise and prudent, and hast revealed them unto babes. Even so, Father: for so it seemed good in thy sight. All things are delivered unto me of my Father: and no man knoweth the Son, but the Father; neither knoweth any man the Father, save the Son, and he to whomsoever the Son reveal him. Matthew 11:25-27

> And, behold, there was a man in Jerusalem, whose name was Simeon; and the same man was just and devout,

waiting for the consolation of Israel: and the Holy Ghost was upon him. And it was revealed unto him by the Holy Ghost, that he should not see death, before he had seen the Lord's Christ. Luke 2:25-26

In that hour Jesus rejoiced in spirit and said, I thank thee, O Father, Lord of heaven and earth, that thou hast hid these things from the wise and prudent, and hast revealed them unto babes; even so, Father; for so it seemed good in thy sight. All things are delivered unto me of my Father: and no man knoweth who the Son is, but the Father; and who the Father is, but the Son, and he to whom the Son will reveal him. And he turned him unto his disciples, and said privately, Blessed are the eyes which see the things that ye see: for I tell you, that man prophets and kings have desired to see those things which ye see, and have not seen them; and to hear those things which ye hear, and have not heard them. Luke 10:21-24

For there is nothing covered, that shall not be revealed; neither hid, that shall not be known. Luke 12:2

If I do not the works of my Father, believe me not. But if I do, though ye believe not me, believe the works; that ye may know, and believe, that the Father is in me, and I in him. John 10:37-38

For I am not ashamed of the gospel of Christ: for it is the power of God unto salvation to every one that believeth; to the Jew first, and also to the Greek. For therein is the righteousness of God revealed from faith to faith: as it is written, The just shall live by faith. For the wrath of God is revealed from heaven against all ungodliness and unrighteousness of men, who hold the truth in unrighteousness. Romans 1:16-18

For I reckon that the sufferings of this present time are not worthy to be compared with the glory which shall be revealed in us. Romans 8:18

Now to him that is of power to stablish you according to my gospel, and the preaching of Jesus Christ, according to the revelation of the mystery, which was kept secret since the world began, But now is made manifest, and by the scriptures of the prophets, according to the commandment of the everlasting God, made known to all nations for the obedience of faith: To God only wise, be glory through Jesus Christ for ever. Romans 16:25-27

But we speak the wisdom of God in a mystery, even the hidden wisdom, which God ordained before the world unto our glory. Which none of the princes of this world knew: for had they known it, they would not have crucified the Lord of glory. But as it is written, Eye hath not seen, nor ear heard, neither have entered into the heart of man, the things which God hath prepared for them that love him. But God hath revealed them unto us by His Spirit: for the Spirit searcheth all things, yea, the deep things of God. For what man knoweth the things of a man, save the spirit of man which is in him? even so the things of God knoweth no man, but the Spirit of God. Now we have received, not the spirit of the world, but the spirit which is of God; that we might know the things that are freely given to us of God. Which things also we speak, not in the words which man's wisdom teacheth, but which the Holy Ghost teacheth: comparing spiritual things with spiritual.
1 Corinthians 2:7-13

Now brethren, if I come unto you speaking with tongues, what shall I profit you, except I shall speak to you either by revelation, or by knowledge, or by prophesying, or by doctrine? 1 Corinthians 14:6

But when it pleased God, who separated me from my mother's womb, and called me by his grace, To reveal his Son in me, that I might preach him among the heathen...
Galatians 1:15-16

But before faith came, we were kept under the law, shut up unto the faith which should afterwards be revealed.
Galatians 3:23

For this cause I Paul, the prisoner of Jesus Christ for you Gentiles, If ye have heard of the dispensation of the grace of God, which is given me to you-ward: How that by revelation he made known unto me the mystery; as I wrote afore in few words, Whereby, when ye read, ye may understand my knowledge in the mystery of Christ, Which in other ages was not made known unto the sons of men, as it is now revealed unto his holy apostles and prophets by the Spirit; that the Gentiles should be fellow heirs, and of the same body, and partakers of his promise in Christ by the gospel: Whereof I was made a minister, according to the gift of the grace of God given unto me by the effectual working of his power. Ephesians 3:1-7

Let us therefore, as many as be perfect, be thus minded: and if any thing ye be otherwise minded, God shall reveal even this unto you. Philippians 3:15

Blessed be the God and Father of our Lord Jesus Christ, which according to his abundant mercy hath begotten us again unto a lively hope by the resurrection of Jesus Christ from the dead. To an inheritance incorruptible, and undefiled, and that fadeth not away, reserved in heaven for you, Who are kept by the power of God through faith unto salvation ready to be revealed in the last time.
1 Peter 1:3-5

Whom having not seen, ye love; in whom, though now ye see him not, yet believing, ye rejoice with joy unspeakable and full of glory: Receiving the end of your faith, even the salvation of your souls. Of which salvation the prophets inquired and searched diligently, who prophesied of the grace that should come unto you: Searching what, or what manner of time the Spirit of Christ which was in them did signify, when it testified beforehand the suffering of Christ, and the glory that should follow. Unto whom it was revealed that not unto themselves, but unto us they did minster the things, which are now reported unto you by them that have preached the gospel unto you with the Holy Ghost sent down from heaven; which things the angels desire to look into. Wherefore gird up the loins of your mind, be sober, and hope to the end for the grace that is to be brought unto you at the revelation of Jesus Christ. 1 Peter 1:8-13

Let us look at a review of the key Truths about *revelation* in these verses.

The Father hid these things, and revealed them unto babes. The Son reveals the Father. Matthew 11:25-27

Holy Ghost was upon him. Luke 2:25

Blessed are the eyes…see those things which ye see…hear those things which ye hear (parable within the parable). Luke 10:24

nothing covered, nothing hid…revealed and known. Luke 12:2

that you may know, and believe…Father in me, I in him. John 10:38

therein is the righteousness of God revealed. Romans 1:17

the glory which shall be revealed in us. Romans 8:18

according to the revelation of the mystery. Romans 16:25

we speak God's wisdom, hidden wisdom, in a mystery...God has revealed them to us by His Spirit...that we may know His wisdom. 1 Corinthians 2:7,10,12

Except I speak to you by revelation, or by knowledge, or by prophesying, or by doctrine. 1 Corinthians 14:6

revealed his Son in me. Galatians 1:16

faith was revealed after the law. Galatians 3:23

the mystery of Christ was made known to Paul by revelation, and is now revealed to all. Ephesians 3:3-5

like-minded, otherwise minded, God shall reveal even this unto you. Philippians 3:15

we are kept by the power of God through faith (His Life) unto salvation ready to be revealed in the last time. 1 Peter 1:5

this salvation was revealed to prophets who inquired, and to us, and reported unto you by those who preached the gospel unto you by the Holy Ghost. 1 Peter 1:8-13

Again, and again, and again...mysteries, as God has revealed them and made known unto us. Are you ready for a spiritual journey to discover some special mysteries God has reserved for those today who seek, and those He has gifted with His Holy Mind?

The Revelation of God
What a special treasure for His Saints.

chapter 2

What is a Parable?

All these things spake Jesus unto the multitudes in parables;
and without a parable spake he not unto them.
Matthew 13:34

With revelation can come the noticing, awareness, and understanding of the greatest mysteries in the Holy Scriptures. Let it be known from the start that one of the greatest mysteries in all of history is the compilation of the Word of God. It has been described in all sorts of ways, often by someone speaking out of the *natural mind.* Ironically God says that mind is *blind, cannot see Truth, cannot receive the things of the Holy Spirit...they are foolishness to that mind, and cannot know them for they are Spiritually discerned* (2 Corinthians 4:3-4; 1 Corinthians 2:14). Wow! That mind thinking it is telling us about the Holy Scriptures.

The world likes to speak of many words/verses as being a simile, metaphor, allegory, fable, metonymy, myth, parody, hyperbole, legend, or enigmatic...anything to take us away from God's Word: *parable.*

Amazingly, God has told us HE has directed the Holy Scriptures to be written in parabolic form. His Word in parables, as such. He spoke not of Spiritual Truth except in parables. Not the physical earthly things: ground, air, clouds, water, earthsuits, animals, food, etc., etc., etc. But all the Spiritual things in the Scriptures.

Here is where the whole Truth of what is a *parable* begins to unfold, and how it plays into reading and understanding the Holy Scriptures. Without knowing all Spiritual Truth is taught in parabolic form, Saints can miss God's teaching most often, if not always. IF Spiritual Truth is seen, it is simply a gift of God without recognizing that.

Definition: A *parable* is *Heavenly Truth with Heavenly meaning.* Period. It is not what most have been taught: an earthly story with a heavenly meaning. Nothing Spiritual in the Holy Scriptures has an earthly source...all Heavenly, all of God. And all Spiritual Truth points to God, never to man/earth/world, etc.

With a faulty (hence, false) definition of a *parable,* Truth can scarcely be known. Only a humanistic reasoning coming from a source other than

God. Hence, a lot of what is taught as Truth is mere humanistic reasoning. And the Saints are powerless for a lack of Truth. Truth is what MAKES us what we need. Truth GIVES us all our need. Truth leaves us with NO want.

In one of the most incredible and enlightening passages in all of the Holy Scriptures, God gives us profound Truth that shakes the foundation of many lives. It can be shocking to find that God spoke in parables so multitudes would not understand or grasp what He was saying. And could not know Truth. Look carefully at the following verses from the record of the first parable noted as such in the first book of the New Testament:

> And he spake many things unto them in parables, saying, Behold, a sower went forth to sow; And when he had sowed, some seeds fell by the way side, and the fowls came and devoured them up: Some fell upon stony places, where they had not much earth: and forthwith they sprung up, because they had no deepness of earth: And when the sun was up, they were scorched. and because they had no root, they withered away. And some fell among the thorns; and the thorns sprung up, and choked them: But other fell into good ground, and brought forth fruit, some an hundredfold, some sixtyfold, some thirtyfold. Who hath ears to hear, let him hear. Matthew 13:3-9

Let us pause for a moment. Do you see that last sentence? Who listening to Jesus did not have ears? Every earth being has ears. Albeit they are physical ears. Therein is an indication of what Jesus was getting at. We will find out about *spiritual ears* very soon. For now, we continue...

> And the disciples came, and said unto him, Why speakest thou unto them in parables? He answered and said unto them, Because it is given unto you to know the mysteries of the kingdom of heaven, but unto them it is not given. For whosoever hath, to him shall be given, and he shall have more abundance: but whosoever hath not, from him shall be taken away even that he hath. Therefore I speak to them in parables because they seeing see not; and hearing they hear not, neither do they understand. And in them is fulfilled the prophecy of Isaiah, which saith, By hearing ye shall hear, and shall not understand, and seeing

ye shall see, and shall not perceive: For this people's heart is waxed gross, and their ears are dull of hearing, and their eyes they have closed; lest at any time they should see with their eyes, and hear with their ears, and should understand with their heart, and should be converted, and I should heal them. But blessed are your eyes, for they see, and your ears, for they hear. For verily I say unto you, That many prophets and righteous men have desired to see those things which ye see, and have not seen them; and to hear those things which ye hear, and have not heard them. Matthew 13:10-17

And then Jesus went on to say, *Hear ye therefore the parable of the sower.* And He then explained the parable to them.

Did any of this grab your attention? Truth get revealed? See what is missing from so many of God's children even to this day? I will never forget the moment I saw that Jesus was saying He spoke in parables so those hearing without Holy ears could not hear. Wow! Could not, would not, and never know Truth. That is amazing.

Throughout this book we will see many instances and ways God has hidden Truth and yet made it available to all His Saints who know and understand about the makeup of a Saint. But, again, let us take a look at some things that guide us toward that incredible discovery.

Look at a couple of parables that are easily recognizable. God identified some directly… although the Heavenly Truth with Heavenly meaning can only be known in the Supernatural, Spiritual Mind of God.

Matthew 13:3-9, *And he spake many things unto them in parables, saying, Behold, a sower went forth to sow…* (v. 3 only).

Matthew 13:24-30, *Another parable put he forth unto them, Saying…* (v. 24 only)

And then, some are not identified with the words like *another parable Jesus spoke,* but are clearly of a different source than any physical statement. Hence, these are impossible to know and discern in the natural or carnal mind. These can only be known in the Mind of God. Think about these. Have they ever given you any difficulty?

Romans 7:15-17, *For that which I do, I allow not: for what I would, that do I not: but what I hate, that do I. If then I do that which I would not, I consent unto the law that it is good. Now then it is no more I that do it, but sin dwelleth in me.*

Ephesians 4:22-24, *That ye put off concerning the former conversation the old man, which is corrupt according to the deceitful lusts; And be renewed in the spirit of your mind; And that ye put on the new man, which after God is created in righteousness and true holiness.*

Finally, there are many Spiritual statements of Truth that are nowhere near identifiable as being parabolic. They may actually appear to be clearly known and understood, but the practice of not casting pearls before the swine leaves these words still hidden from any other than the Mind of God.

Galatians 2:20, *I am crucified with Christ: nevertheless I live; yet not I, but Christ liveth in me: and the life which I now live in the flesh I live by the faith of the Son of God, who loved me, and gave himself for me.*

Colossians 1:26-27, *Even the mystery which hath been hid from ages and from generations, but is now made manifest to his saints: To whom God would make known what is the riches of the glory of this mystery among the Gentiles; which is Christ in you, the hope of glory.*

So, buckle up and prepare to see some things (hopefully, See some things) that have been hidden for far too long from many Saints of God. Think on these thoughts as we bring this first chapter to a close...

I have found it difficult to be thinking in the carnal mind and be alert to what sinners are thinking. Soak on that a bit. We will answer that dilemma before we are through.

All of this sets the cornerstone for delving into what is a *spiritual soul?* The *spiritual soul* is one of the three key parts of *beings* that gives the function *of the being* in whatever *suit* the being resides. We will identify those three parts and their importance a little later in the book.

Once we know what a *spiritual soul* is then we can begin to think about where the soul is located in the being, the entity of the soul, the spirituality of the soul, and the function of the soul. All are an amazing creation of God in earth beings. In fact, to understand the reality of living we must understand all these things about the *spiritual soul*.

But first, we must understand some other foundational premises that also undergird and prepare us to know and grasp God's parabolic Truth about the two souls of a Saint.

chapter 3

Make Disciples

And Jesus came and spake unto them, saying,
All power is given unto me in heaven and in earth.
Go ye therefore, and teach all nations, baptizing them
in the name of the Father, and of the Son, and of the Holy Ghost.
Teaching them to observe all things whatsoever I have commanded you:
and lo, I am with you always, even unto the end of the world.
Matthew 28:18-20

In one of Jesus' most direct and bold commands to His disciples, He tells them these things (combining physical and parabolic Spiritual words). This concluded the Book of Matthew. Look at the key points:

- Jesus speaking, with all power in heaven and in earth
- go ye therefore
- teach all to observe all things I have commanded
- baptize (have them give a witness of their salvation)
- Jesus is with His Saints always, everywhere, forever

Couple this with Jesus' telling His disciples that He only spoke in parables, we must know from the start that Spiritual Truth in the Holy Scriptures is of parabolic teaching, and literally taking the Scriptures without thinking parabolically in the Mind of God misses the Truth of God. This is a tough saying.

Therefore, let us begin with thinking about some of Jesus' parabolic premises in Matthew to get us in the Mind of God prepared to See the Heavenly Truth with a Heavenly meaning when we get to the actual parabolic teaching of the two (2) souls.

Who was Jesus? He was God. Therefore, we must be parabolically thinking when we see Who Jesus was when He came to the disciples and spoke to them. And when we see the three of the Triune God mentioned (or, two in some cases), this is speaking of the One God in His three different manifestations.

In the natural or carnal minds so many argue that there are 3 Gods. Not So. One God, three Personal manifestations (even at the same time).

We cannot forget why God tells us He always speaks in parables. So, *they* won't understand. They being sinners in their natural mind and Saints in our carnal mind. This has be to be known, understood, received, and owned. Saints cannot move forward in Truth without knowing these two spiritual minds exist. And both exist in each Saint. And one cannot grasp Truth.

One more thing. The words *teaching them to observe* are a great parabolic phrase. To the carnal mind these seem to say we teach the new disciples what they must *do*...observe all the teachings, commands, etc. But the Holy Mind of God in us knows *all these things* can only be done by God Himself. Holy Spirit IN all Saints.

The physical things in these three verses can be carried out in a Saint's physical earthsuit by the Saint. We decide whether we will hear God's words to go, teach, and baptize. Saints decide to *do* the physical things while depending entirely on *God to do/accomplish* the Spiritual things.

Anyone not believing this or thinking this is not God's Way should abandon whatever way the Spiritual has been tried, and watch to see if God will do the Spiritual in you. That is a sweet abandonment to Him. When *God does* the Spiritual great Spiritual power is upon the *doing*.

Therefore one of the first things to teach anyone in *making a disciple* is *the parable of the two souls, two minds*. With what we will know from the entirety of this book, we can know and see God doing this through us.

chapter 4

What Is A Foundation?

Whosoever cometh to me, and heareth my sayings,
and doeth them, I will show you to whom he is like:
He is like a man which built an house, and digged deep,
and laid the foundation on a rock: and when the
flood arose, the stream beat vehemently upon that house,
and could not shake it; for it was founded upon a rock.
Luke 6:47-48

A foundation is that which all other is built upon. We are very familiar with the foundation of homes, larger buildings, and very large sky-scraper buildings. We know that without the proper foundation those structures could not stand up very long. But, herein is a major parabolic statement from Christ.

What is dealt with in this book is kin to the premise of the words in Isaiah 28:9-10,

Whom shall he teach knowledge? and whom shall he make
to understand doctrine? them that are weaned from the
milk, and drawn from the breasts. For precept must be
upon precept, precept upon precept; line upon line, line
upon line; here a little, and there a little.

It all boils down to one thing. Begin with a Truth. The foundation. Add another Truth, then another. Practically speaking we call these a premise. As my friend Jesse says, "to know truth we have to get back to our last premise." A premise being the last Truth we have known that was revealed and established.

Another parabolic Truth to consider…God has told us He is building us into a *house. The House of God.*

But Christ as a son over his own house; whose house are
we… Hebrews 3:6

It is the same for Christianity and all humanity. God designed the creation of Adam & Eve, man and woman, with a foundation for His House that would last for eternity. Three parts. It takes knowing all that is in this book to really see and understand how each part of every life plays a role in eternity.

Also, God Himself has the same basic foundation. Three parts. We will find these in the chapters to follow. With His trichotomy (3 parts) it is not difficult to see why God created mankind with the same construct.

We must never forget to look for the trichotomy of every individual being. These three parts hold the Truth of existence, experience, and eternity. Existence, who we are. Experience, how we live. Eternity, what we will be like forever (after our physical death).

Can you think of the three parts of your trichotomy without looking further into this book? Can you believe that knowing your trichotomy, and that of everyone else, can impact every thought, word, and action you should take?

It is important for us to know these things. They affect the totality of our life experiences. They are the ingredients of every Saint's foundation.

chapter 5

Ingredients of a Saint's Foundation

But ye are not in the flesh, but in the Spirit,
if so be that the Spirit of God dwell in you.
Now if any man have not the Spirit of Christ,
he is none of his.
Romans 8:9

For the word of God is quick, and powerful,
and sharper than any two-edged sword,
piercing even to the dividing asunder
of soul and spirit, and of the joints and marrow,
and is a discerner of the thoughts and intents of the heart.
Hebrews 4:12

What? know ye not that your body
is the temple of the Holy Ghost which is in you,
which ye have of God, and ye are not your own?
For ye are bought with a price:
therefore glorify God in your body,
and in your spirit, which are God's.
1 Corinthians 6:19-20

The foundational premise of a Saint's structure greatly impacts the life of every Saint.

In fact, the ingredients of a Saint's foundation have a greater impact on everything a Saint thinks, speaks, and does beyond what most ever consider. Without knowing these ingredients, how could a Saint begin to function properly with these important parts?

If we do not know we have something, how often are we likely to use it? How often would we work to make changes, improve, or preserve it? In this case, the *it* is a *them*. The three parts of the trichotomy of a Saint. Many spiritual trichotomy diagrams are found in this book. These will give us greater insight into the makeup of a trichotomy in various manifestations.

As you might imagine, we will look with great detail for the rest of the book at these three parts. For now let us discover what they are.

First, every Saint has a body. I like to call it our *earthsuit*. Primarily because that distinguishes it from what Scripture calls the *body of Christ*. Which references to the totality of the number of Saints. All of the Saints make up the *body of Christ*. Our *earthsuit* is our physical body for life on earth. Each individual, sinner and Saint, will get an *eternal suit,* be it a *hell-suit* or a *Heaven-suit.*

Second, every Saint has a Spirit. God's Word is clear in telling us that Holy Spirit is our Spirit. As a sinner, we had unholy spirit, the consequence of Adam & Eve's sin in the Garden. God has given us a beautiful verse that specifies the importance of Saints having Holy Spirit.

> But ye are not in the flesh, but in the Spirit, if so be that
> the Spirit of God dwell in you. Now if any man have not
> the Spirit of Christ, he is none of his. Romans 8:9

Holy Spirit through the pen of the Apostle Paul definitely says every Saint has Holy Spirit. If a person does not, they are not a Saint. Pretty uncomplicated, isn't it. Does that give us any idea of the importance of knowing this part of a trichotomy? Absolutely. And it is important to know that denying self is a work of Holy Spirit.

Third, every Saint has a soul. In fact, two souls. This is the need and reason for this book. This is where things can get a little complex. Not complicated, but a little bit more than simple. Sinners have one soul. God designed a Saint to have two souls. For two good reasons. One is so that a Saint on earth would be different from Jesus on earth. Jesus had one soul. His Holy Soul. When a sinner becomes a Saint, Holy Soul is imparted to the new Saint. If a Saint did not have 2 souls (only Holy Soul), we would be exactly as Jesus was when He walked this earth.

Number two is our still having the residue unholy, natural soul makes us dependent upon God for almost everything. Especially anything and everything Spiritual. The diagrams will picture this for you more clearly. Unholy soul, not unholy spirit. Life is in the spirit. It is in the soul that we experience life. Saints experience the Righteousness and the Life of God from Holy Soul, and experience the sinfulness and naturalness from the residue unholy, natural soul.

It is important to know that each soul has three parts that form the *heart* of an individual. These three are mind, emotions, and will. The sum of the actions of these three form the heart of the person. As you would think, this heart is a spiritual heart, different from the physical heart in the earthsuit which pumps blood and oxygen throughout the earthsuit.

Be sure to note a Saint has two spiritual hearts. This plays a big part in evaluating the working of each soul in a Saint.

A great number of times the *soul*, the *mind*, the *emotions*, the *will*, and the *heart* are mentioned throughout both testaments. Here is a brief reference of verses to look at to see how God shows the function of the totality of our soul and heart.

mind – Proverbs 2:10; Lamentations 3:20; Romans 8:7; Philippians 2:2

emotions – Psalm 42:1; Psalm 86:4; Judges 10:16; Job 30:25; John
14:27, 15:11

will – Job 6:7; Job 7:15; 1 Chronicles 22:19; 2 Timothy 3:12

If you want to thrill your Heart (the Heart of God in you), do an expanded word search in an exhaustive concordance!

Everything spiritual in our earthsuit (Saint) depends on which mind's thoughts are being lived.

We will have chapters that give much more information about these parts. But, again, these are very important for a Saint to know in order to function as God originally planned for His Saint to Live.

I think you will find the information to follow to be of great use and great exhilaration in your life.

chapter 6

Words Have Meaning
Say What You Mean & Mean What You Say

Therefore if I know not the meaning of the voice,
I shall be unto him that speaketh a barbarian,
and he that speaketh shall be a barbarian unto me.
1 Corinthians 14:12

Nothing can inhibit communication like a faulty (false) or incorrect word. Far too often a little carelessness in knowing a correct definition of a Scriptural word and believing a false definition detours a Saint from hearing from God. This is why we must be very careful to know and to use God's words God's way.

We rise and fall by our definitions of words. How a word is defined tells us exactly what that word is. The key word is *is*. What is *is?* Whatever is on one side of the word *is* is equal to the other side of the word *is*.

In any statement saying *God is love,* God equals love. God *is* love. Love is not an attribute of God, God *is* Him. That *is* Who God *is*. He *is* Love. When we speak of the *Grace of God,* that is a different story. The Grace of God is talking about something that God *does*. It is *an unmerited favor of God* to us, but what isn't?

The Grace of God is the *doing* of God, the *working* of God. Grace is an action of God, not *Who* He *is*. God *is* Faith. Faith *is* an ultimate revealing of His Life. Scriptural Faith *is* the Life of God. His Life expresses Himself by *doing,* and doing *is* His Grace.

My Dad was a math teacher and coach. From an early age he taught me *is* means *equals*. In math, as in all of life, what is on one side of the equal sign *is* the same as what *is* on the other side of the equal sign. That's just what *is* or equals is. Either side cannot be different than the other side.

When we say something *is* another thing, we must know we are saying the two *are* equal, the same. Absolutely the same as. No difference whatsoever. And if the two sayings on both sides of the *is* are not the same, we have therefore given an error or falsehood.

God initiated this whole Truth when He said *I am*. *I am* is the same thing as saying *I is*. But English teachers teach us the correct term to use is *am,* but *am* means the *same* as *is*.

What is remarkable to know and understand is that the Spiritual Life of a Saint *is* God. *I* have been crucified, yet *I* live, Who *is* doing, or to do, the Spiritual Living in and through a Saint's earthsuit? God. God tells us Spiritually there *is* no more *I* (the old man) around. It *is* God. He *is*.

Think about Paul's statement (actually Holy Spirit speaking through Paul), *But by the grace of God I am what I am: and his grace which was bestowed upon me was not in vain; but I labored more abundantly than they all: yet not I, but the grace of God which was with me* (1 Corinthians 15:10). Hooooo-boy!

Isn't it exciting to See the Truth with the Spiritual Eyes and understand with the Spiritual Mind! *Grace* and *I* become alive and real in the Mind of God therein. A parabolic statement is not seen, nor known, nor understood in the natural/carnal mind. A parable or parabolic teaching are often greatly misunderstood. This can cause any one of us living in the carnal mind to miss one of the greatest Truths in all of Scripture: ALL Spiritual Truth is given parabolically by God in the Holy Scriptures. We will see this clearly before we are through.

So all of this applies then to the Truth that faulty definitions or false definitions give us a false idea of who or what *is*. These definitions cause us to *fall from Truth*.

Remember, we rise and fall with our definitions. Therefore as we study the Word of God, to get to the bottom line of Truth about all people or things, *(and here we are talking about 2 souls in this book)* we must get to and know the correct words that God used and the correct Scriptural definitions that God used. A truthful definition is a foundational premise for moving forward in understanding what God is saying to us.

In Chapter 7 we will see several key words that are foundational Scripture words with their important Scriptural definitions.

I have come to the point of knowing the absolute Truth can only be known in the original languages. That is why we will see many Greek words herein.

chapter 7

Mini-Dictionary of Key Words

Hold fast the form of sound words,
which thou hast heard of me,
in faith and love which is Christ Jesus.
That good thing which was committed unto thee
keep by the Holy Ghost which dwelleth in us.
2 Timothy 1:13-14

Thou therefore, my son, be strong
in the grace that is in Christ Jesus...
Study to show thyself approved unto God,
a workman that needeth not to be ashamed,
rightly dividing the word of truth.
2 Timothy 2:1, 15

To understand Scripture, we must know several key words that provide the undergirding of the foundational fundamental Truths of the Holy Scriptures. Of which many are the premise of the Truths presented in this book. The following are a list, with definitions, of these important words gathered together for convenient reference.

There are a lot of Scriptural words carelessly thrown around in spiritual circles that have the Saints of God chasing false ideas. False definitions is one of the most prevalent ways our enemy distorts, deceives, and detours us from God's Truth. The original languages of the original texts of the Old Testament and New Testament are the only words which give Saints Truth. A correct translation into a native language sounds good, but even there many words have a different meaning than they did years before, or will have years later than now.

Seeking to know the original language words from a reputable and reliable source is sometimes quite a challenge. Scriptural Truth is the best commentary for all Scriptures. Therefore, it is excellent to search different references for confirmation of the Scriptural meaning of even the original text words. I heard one recognized as a Greek (and Hebrew) expert (the go-to source for 1,000's of preachers and Bible students), at his age 85, say, "I was born on the island of Cyprus. I have studied the Greek language for 75 years. And I am still learning the Greek language." That's encouraging, isn't it.

But we cannot afford to fail to search and study original languages and their accurate translations into our native language. The Truth of the Holy Scriptures demands it. The following are several key, important words appearing in this book.

Arranged in alphabetical order
(some words are capitalized…indicating the Life of God)

- **begat** – Heb. *yalad* Gr. *gennao*
  The method of conception and birth by which all earth beings have come into being since the Fall of Adam & Eve. Only Adam & Eve were created, by God.

- **believe** – Gr. *pisteuo*
  To have knowledge and to commit to or assent to, to trust, more than a mental act (includes a moral action), when God talks us into some Truth. Believe is the one command/imperative God tells us is our main responsibility. Legalism (works) detours, diminishes, and defeats God's primary instruction. Believe is only mentioned 19 times in 17 verses in the O.T., 124 times in the N.T.

- **Believers/Christians/Saints** – Gr. *hagios.* (for Saints only)
  Believer does not appear in Scripture. *Believers* appears 2 times (Acts 5:14; 1 Timothy 4:12). Same Greek word as *believe*.
  Christian appears 2 times (Acts 26:28; 1 Peter 4:16). *Christians* appears 1 time (Acts 11:26). This is shocking, isn't it? The term for the name virtually all Born Again Believers use to call each other. Interestingly, it is not a name used by Christians themselves in the N.T. These terms are used by others referring to *followers of Christ.*
  Saint appears only 1 time in the N.T. (Philippians 4:21). *Saints* appears 62 times in the N.T. (a form of *Saints* appears 101 times in Scripture. THIS is the name God gives for His children to be called. Why? The name *(hagios)* means holy. A holy person. Believing God's Way makes us one of God's *Saints.*

- **create** – Heb. *bara*

   To bring something into being that has never before existed. That which only God can do. It does not mean to take something, or two or more somethings, and make something new.

   created – Gr. *ktizo*

   The English *create* does not appear in the N.T. Only *created*. Past tense for *create*. 12 times in N.T. Every time referring to that which only God has done.

- **crucified life** – Gr. *stauroo zoe*

   The old spiritual life of a sinner is crucified at the salvation of a repentant individual. This life exists no more in that individual. It is often misrepresented as the life of a Saint, which is the New Creation Life (Spiritual Life).

- **earthsuit/body/flesh** – Gr. *soma/sarx*

   (earthsuit is not in Scripture)

   This is my term for the earthly body. I use it to differentiate other times *body (soma)* or *flesh (sarx)* are mentioned with a different meaning. And to point to its specific temporary limitation for housing spirit & soul on earth.

   Body has other meanings in Scripture than to identify an earth being's earthsuit. From the Greek *soma*.

   Flesh more often carries the meaning of *that which is opposed to God* instead of referring to an earth being's *earthsuit*. From the Greek *sarx*. To walk in the *flesh* is to walk in the *carnal soul* and its carnal mind/emotions/will/heart that are under the controlling influence of the devil. This is the enemy that presents the battle with Holy Soul in Saints. The battle is never in the Spirit (Holy Spirit) of a Saint.

- **eternal life** – Gr. *aionios zoe*

   Everlasting or never ending existence. It is interesting that most generally refer to the Eternal Life of a Saint when mentioning this term. However, it is also said by most that sinners will spend an eternity in Hell. But that is not often referred to as an eternal life…yet it is everlasting.

- **Faith** – Gr. *pistis*

    Faith only appears 2 times in the O.T. 245 times in the N.T. A crucial word for Life as a Saint. Key point: God tells us Faith (His Supernatural Spiritual Life) is Fruit of Holy Spirit. The Source of Faith is God Himself. Not of our doing. To have Scriptural Faith is to have the Life of God.

    Too many co-mingle *faith* with *believe*. These are two different Greek words with two totally different sources and meanings. Believe leads to Faith. Holy Spirit seals a Saint's believing when He knows we have committed our trust to Truth.

- **Fruit of the vine/tree** – Gr. *karpos*

    The *fruit* is a manifestation of the *life* of the vine/tree. In fact, the ultimate manifestation of the *life*. Apple trees produce apples. Tomato vines produce tomatoes. The *life* of the vine/tree flows through the vine/tree and culminates in its *fruit. Fruit* is *life*.

- **Fruit of the Holy Spirit** – Gr. *karpos*

    This *Fruit* is *Life* (with a capital F and capital L). *Life* of Holy Spirit. *His Life* flowing through Saints produces *Supernatural Spiritual Fruit*. A lot of people look at *works* and call them *fruit*. Most of the time they are looking at *fleshly works. Fruit of the Holy Spirit* can only be called such when originated by the *Life* that Holy Spirit has produced/does. God is the Source.

    This is one of the hidden parabolic treasures of the New Testament.

- **good & evil** – Gr. *kalos* and *poneros*.

    These two words Scripturally come from *the tree of the knowledge of good and evil* in Genesis 2:9. It was the tree God forbid Adam & Eve to eat from. *Good* is a word that many embrace as being from God. Not so. *Good* cannot compare with Righteousness, and is used as a pitiful counterfeit. In fact, the Lord Jesus said that God

34

alone was *good* without limitation or qualification and added, *why callest thou me good?* (Mark 10:18; Luke 18:19). That should be enough to know that *good* is a word we need to be careful about using. Good might be benevolent, but not always. Evil is always evil. *Righteousness* is God's word, instead of *good*.

It is important to know that there is no limit to the extreme of good or evil that the natural/carnal minds can think and lead into an action. That tells us a lot about the thoughts and actions of the sinners and some Saints.

- **Grace of God** – Gr. *charis*.

  One of the most important words for Saints to know and understand. The meaning has been distorted and detoured by the devil to render it a weak, nebulous word when it is one that speaks of the mighty power of God. Very simply, Grace (of God) is God's doing, God's working. It is an unmerited favor, but God's Grace is the power which delivers the favor in all instances. A Saint can enjoy all the wonderful works of God when reading Scripture and seeing all is by His Grace. Which, by the way, what do Saints have that is not unmerited (or, looking at it differently, is merited)? Grace is to be freely received from the great *mercy* of God.

- **heart** – Gr. *kardia*

  Everyone knows about the physical heart, but Scripture speaks of a spiritual heart. This is a case where thinking in the spiritual is very important. Analogy of Scripture (letting Scripture be the best commentary on Scripture) gives us the knowledge of the spiritual heart being the sum of the working of the three parts of the soul (mind, emotions, will). The heart reflects the totality of the soul's functioning.

- **humanism** – (there is no such word in Scripture. Neither is **human.**) Both are counterfeit words from the devil. Humanism is a term for *man's way of thinking and worshipping*. It is actually the religion of *man is god*. The term *human* is a counterfeit of the devil

35

to distract, diminish, and detour from all the terms God has given and used for earth beings, sinners and Saints.

- **image** – Heb. *tselem;* Gr. *eikon.*
  Interestingly, *tselem* appears 16 times in the O.T., 5 times referring to an earthly being. The other 11 times referring to idols. It simply means an image, resemblance, illusion, or representative figure. *Tselem* does not mean an exact duplicate. However in the case of a Born Again Saint there are two Spiritual parts of our trichotomy that ARE the exact duplicate of God's *likeness.* Holy Spirit and Holy Soul. Knowing and understanding the totality of that is important. The Greek, *eikon,* is used the same in the N.T.

- **life / Life** – Heb. *chay* Gr. *zoe*
  Living. Alive. Being. There is no difference in the Hebrew and the Greek words when speaking of physical life, natural life, carnal spiritual life, or Supernatural Spiritual Life. Yet there is a great difference when *living* or *Living* in one or the other. Spiritually, one is of the devil (lowercase *l*) and one is of God (capital *L*).
  I think it very important to recognize and know about the two different lives spoken of. To differentiate the parabolic teachings. Each has a vastly different eternal destiny. And a vastly different impact on existence here on earth. Genesis 2:9, Tree of Life, is the first mention of the Life of God in Scripture.
  More about this tree is found under Tree of Life.

- **likeness** – Heb. *demuwth*; Gr. - *homoioma*
  The state or quality of being similar, like another. The same form, shape, or contents. A copy. A duplicate.
  The likeness of God or Adam is referring to being of a like physical/spiritual similarity with three parts – spirit, soul, body. This identifies earth beings with God more than image.
  Likeness does not have to be exactness of details, but similar in makeup.

- **Mind of God** – Gr. *nous theos*

  The Supernatural Spiritual Mind of God is the Omniscient Mind God possesses. There is no limit to the knowledge and Spirituality of His Mind. In 1 Corinthians 2:16 a Saint is said to possess the Mind of God. Very few ever believe this.

- **natural/carnal mind** – Gr. *psuchikos sarx phronema*

  To be carnally spiritually minded. To mind the things of the flesh (that which is enmity with God). The natural mind is the mind of the sinner from birth. The carnal mind is the same mind in a Saint, but in Scripture is called the carnal mind (location: unholy soul).

  This mind originated with Adam & Eve eating of the forbidden tree of the knowledge of good and evil in the Garden of Eden.

- **New Creature** – Gr. *kainos ktisis*

  2 Corinthians 5:17 tells us that at salvation, the New Saint is in Christ, a new creature, all (Spiritual) things are new. Grasping the difference between the Spiritual new and something not changing in the physical is the difference between a Saint functioning in the Mind of God or functioning in the carnal mind. Carnal Saints tend to see and think of the physical changes instead of the Spiritual changes.

- **Parable** – Gr. *parabole*

  Heavenly Truth with Heavenly meaning, sometimes using earthly illustrations (but not all that often).
  - Matthew 13:1-9 (to the multitudes), 13:10-23 (to a few disciples), and 13:34-35 (to the multitudes) are the prime teachings about parables.
  - Also in Mark 4:1-9 (to the multitudes), 4:10-34 (to a few disciples).

- **physical brain** – (neither word appears in Scripture)

  Since the Holy Scriptures are the Spiritual Word of God that do encompass some physical things, we cannot deny the physical exists or is unknown to the spiritual minds. But the physical brain does not think in the spiritual. It only functions in the physical realm. Knowing physical things.

It is important to know that we should not be trying to see things physically if they are spiritual. Or try to analyze spiritual things with the physical brain. Know the two spiritual souls, the two spiritual minds, and know we choose which one to function out of.

- **revelation** – Gr. *apokalupsis*
  God's revealing of Heavenly Truth with Heavenly meaning. It can be known as an appearing, a manifestation, and to be revealed.

- **Righteous/Righteousness** – Gr. *dikaios/dilaiosune.*
  Right/just. Righteousness is the Holiness of God. *Good* cannot compare with Righteousness, and is used as a pitiful counterfeit. When God's Life is Living through the earthsuit of a Saint, it means a Saint enjoys exhibiting the Life of God instead of earthly, fleshly actions. It is the Holy state God declares every Saint to be from the moment of salvation. It is not a way of life to try and obtain or be like. A Saint cannot earn Righteousness. It is the Life of the Saint. *Good* is no good for a Saint. Only Righteousness.

- **Saints/Christians** – Gr. *hagios*
  Born Again/New Creation of God. Holy Spirit, two souls (Holy Soul & carnal soul), and the same physical earthsuit originally born with.

- **salvation** – Gr. *soteria*
  The forgiveness of ALL sins (past, present, and future) and the eradication of the *sin life* in sinners, but there is the retention of the natural soul and earthsuit. Salvation also includes the giving of the New Creation of a Saint in the same earthsuit (Holy Spirit and Holy Soul). Holy Spirit replaces the unholy spirit.

- **sinners** – Gr. *hamartolos*

  All are spiritually born this way originally due to the consequence of Adam's sin. Sinners have a sinful, Adam spirit. And a natural soul. And a physical earthsuit. Sinners are sinners and sin because of who they are, not because of what they do.

- **soul** – Gr. *psuche*

  The soul of an individual is the spiritual housing of the spiritual mind, emotions, and will. This is Truth for God, Saints (having two souls), and sinners. The soul is where the spiritual functions issue forth from. The Spirit is life. The soul is the function of the mind, emotions, and will (chooser). The heart is the sum of the functioning of these three.

- **spirit / Spirit** – Heb. *ruwach*. Gr. *pneuma*

  Another instance of one Hebrew word and one Greek word for both the unholy spiritual and the Holy Spiritual. The words mean *breath* and *life*. The saying Jesus *gave up the Holy Ghost* means His Spirit departed His earthly body. The same happens at the physical death of all earth beings. To be baptized with the Holy Ghost is to be immersed into the Life of Holy Spirit. The life of a sinner is unholy. The Life of a Saint is Holy. Both lives are in the respective spirits.

- **spiritual blindness** – Gr. *pneumatikos porosis*

  This is a blindness or hardness that exists in the natural or carnal minds. To live in such is to be unable to see Spiritual Truth.

- **spiritual soul** – Gr. *pneumatikos psuche*

  There are two different spiritual souls. One is the soul of the sinner, an unholy gathering of the natural mind, emotions, and will (chooser). The other is the Soul of God and the Soul of His Saints, a Holy gathering of the Holy Mind of God, His Emotions, and His Will (Chooser). The three equaling His Heart.

- **tree of the knowledge of good & evil** – Heb. *'ets . da'ath . kalos . poneros*
From Genesis 2:9. The fruit of this tree God forbid Adam & Eve to eat of. For He knew that the minute they ate of this fruit they would die a spiritual death. They would know *good* and *evil*. They would have that life instead of the innocent life they were created with. This knowledge is a demonic deviation from righteousness in two different forms. *Good* is not righteousness, and certainly *evil* is not. Sadly too many Saints think of *good* as being OK.

- **Tree of Life** – Heb. *chay*
    The Life of this tree is parabolically the Life of God, Eternal Life.
    Scripture never says that God forbid Adam & Eve in their sinless, innocent state to eat of the Tree of Life. Of course, the Omniscient God knew that they wouldn't, not before they ate of the tree of the knowledge of good & evil. After they ate of the forbidden tree, that is when God said,

    > And the Lord God said, Behold the man is become as one of us, to know good and evil: and now, lest he put forth his hand, and take also of the tree of life, and eat, and live for ever: Therefore the Lord God sent him forth from the garden of Eden, to till the ground from when he was taken. So he drove out the man; and he placed at the east of the garden of Eden cherubim, and a flaming sword which turned every way, to keep the way of the tree of life. Genesis 3:22-24

- **trichotomy** – (this word does not appear as such in Scripture). 3 parts. With God and earth beings the three parts are spirit, soul, and body. *(human* is a man-made word, not found in the Holy Scriptures). Earth beings and earthsuit are more scriptural and definitive.
- **Truth** – Gr. *aletheia*

Scriptural Truth may be that which tells of verifiable facts that are not of a spiritual nature. The identification in Scripture of places, people, historical actions, etc. is an example of such.

Scriptural Truth primarily thought of in this book is that which tells of Divine Life. God is Truth. The Lord Jesus said Himself *I am the Truth*. There is no Scriptural Spiritual Truth apart from God.

- **Will of God** – Gr. *thelema theos*

    The Will of God is not a plan. Certainly not a perfect plan. It is a determination or decision/choice based on the inclination or desire/pleasure of the one choosing. It is that which closely ties to the Heart of God. Inside each Saint there is a "chooser switch"…that which decides whether to live in the carnal soul or Holy Soul.

chapter 8

Some Basic Tenets of Christianity

All scripture is given by inspiration of God,
and is profitable for doctrine, for reproof,
for correction, for instruction in righteousness.
That the man of God may be perfect,
thoroughly furnished unto all good works.
2 Timothy 3:16-17

There are basic tenets of the Holy Scriptures that must be known and understood:

1. No earth being can perform or do any Supernatural Spiritual work. Only God can (Father, Son, Holy Spirit).
2. There are only two types of earth beings:
   - sinners
   - Saints (called Christians 3 times in the NT, called Saints 61 times...the latter being the name God calls His children). Saint is from the Greek, *hagios,* meaning holy.

     There is not one instance in the NT of a Saint being someone who has died and is voted on to become a Saint.
3. All Scripture is parabolic when speaking of Spiritual Truth (Galatians 2:20 is a perfect example).
4. There in essence are 4 *minds* a Saint has to think of and deal with. Physical brain, Mind of God, carnal mind (which has two parts: good & evil).
5. Every Saint must know:
   - what it means to be a Saint, and the impact on our days on earth and Eternal Life
   - how to share clearly the way someone becomes a Saint
   - the blindness of the sinner's mind (2 Corinthians 4:3-4; 1 Corinthians 2:14), and the necessity of presenting the Gospel to a sinner.
6. The difference between *image* and *likeness* of Genesis 1:26-27.
   - understanding only Adam & Eve were created earth beings
   - all others since have been begat by their parents

7. A Saint is a new creation (2 Corinthians 5:17 and other verses). There are only two new parts of this creation (Holy Spirit and Holy Soul).
8. In eternity, both sinners and Saints get a new suit (body). Sinners, a hell-suit. Saints, a Heaven-suit.
9. There is no limit to the extreme of ridiculousness the natural and carnal spiritual minds can think. There is no limit spiritually to the extreme that the evil spiritual mind can think (and cause actions). The same with the good spiritual mind. The physical brain does not think spiritually. Both the physical brain and the natural and carnal spiritual minds are the tools of the devil to cause physical/spiritual calamity and spiritual ignorance on earth.
10. The Supernatural Spiritual Mind of God in Saints (same Mind as in God/Jesus/Holy Spirit) can think only Righteousness. This Mind is unlimited in all Spiritual and physical knowledge (the Omniscience of God).

chapter 9

3 is the Key

But I certify you, brethren
that the gospel which was preached
of me is not after man.
For I neither received it of man,
neither was I taught it,
but by the revelation of Jesus Christ.
Galatians 1:12

The same day went Jesus out of the house,
and sat by the sea side.
And great multitudes were gathered together
unto him, so that he went into a ship, and sat;
and the whole multitude stood on the shore.
And he spake many things unto them in parables…
Matthew 13:1-3

And now abideth faith, hope, charity, these three;
but the greatest of these is charity.
1 Corinthians 13:13

There are some fundamental Truths that undergird all Spiritual Truth revealed by God. We must receive these correctly in order to get more Truth. God tells us that no Spiritual Truth can be known apart from these three. They are: *revelation, parables,* and *trichotomies.* These hold the key to why we stand in Truth or errors and false thinking. If we don't get these three, we miss God/Truth/Life. And no Righteousness can come from that. They must be gained in order, precept upon precept.

Let us look at each of these three briefly. They will be mentioned over and over throughout the book, giving more detail as we go along.

revelation – God explicitly tells us that anyone must have the revelation (revealing) from Him in order to know Truth. In fact, to begin to know God (Who is Truth).

No man can come unto me, except the Father which hath
sent me draw him: and I will raise him up at the last day.
John 6:44

Jesus saith unto him, I am the way, the truth, and the life:
no man cometh unto the Father, but by me. If ye had
known me, ye should have known my Father also: and
from henceforth ye know him, and have seen him.
John 14:6-7

Without revelation from God, no one knows Spiritual Truth. God tells us
the explicit way Truth is not known, and known.

But the natural man receiveth not the things of the Spirit
of God: for they are foolishness unto him: neither can he
know them, because they are spiritually discerned.
1 Corinthians 2:14

For who hath known the mind of the Lord, that he may
instruct him? But we have the mind of Christ.
1 Corinthians 2:16

For I know nothing by myself; yet am I not hereby
justified: but he that judgeth me is the Lord...For who
maketh thee to differ from another? and what hast thou
that thou didst not receive? now if thou didst receive it,
why dost thou glory, as if thou hadst not received it?
1 Corinthians 4:4, 7

Now here is something extremely relative to God's revelation. The
actual Words of God. And definitions. Translations are always susceptible
to misinterpretation. Need proof? Look at all the different translations
with differing interpretations in print and available on the market today.
That doesn't even consider the fact of varying *manuscripts (more like the
originals,* so it is said). But, on top of that, one tool of the devil for centuries
has been the *definitions* of words. Not only does he have Saints in the carnal
mind arguing over which is the correct manuscript, but also arguing over
what an English word means (very few ever look at the original languages).
Each Saint should pay attention to which translation we think is God's
Word (it is impossible for two different manuscripts to be THE Word of

God). And, we must give heed to knowing the original languages and the most correct definitions of those words.

If we want to know Truth, we need to pray for God to give His revelation of His Spiritual Truth. This is no small matter. No Truth is known without Divine revelation. Mysteries are made known only by revelation. We will find an abundance of God's revelation throughout this book.

parables – All of God's Spiritual teaching/Truth is revealed through parables, parabolisms, parabolic teaching. God says so. And God gives the explicit reason for using this method to convey Spiritual Truth.

We saw in chapter 2 the *parable of the sower*. And we saw the reason Jesus spoke in parables.

Multitudes have wrestled with these verses for years to try and understand exactly what Jesus was saying. In fact, His closest disciples standing there with Him that day were wrestling with His words. Jesus knew this and later opened and expounded the Truth to them.

The entire Holy Scriptures are chock full of parables and parabolic sayings. It takes careful reading and studying to grasp the Heavenly Truths with Heavenly meanings. But, for now, let me mention 1 thing to always remember:

- Jesus says He speaks in parables so they will not see, hear, or understand. Who is *they?* Those without God's Spiritual Eyes, Ears, and Mind.

Keep this in mind right now: there are many astounding Truths that become known to a Saint who learns to know and appreciate Jesus' teaching in parables.

One other monumental Truth: verses 34-35 of Matthew 13, after Jesus explains the *parable of the sower* to these closest disciples, speaks a parable about the *wheat and the tares,* speaks a parable about *heaven and a grain of mustard seed,* and *speaks a parable about heaven and leaven.*

> All these things spake Jesus unto the multitudes in parables; and without a parable spake he not unto them.
> That it might be fulfilled which was spoken by the prophet, saying, I will open my mouth in parables; I will

utter things which have been kept secret from the foundation of the world.

Without a parable spake he not unto them. Wow! We will see multiple parabolic sayings in this book. God has spoken many things that through the years the vast majority of people have not seen, heard, or understood. Read vs. 10-17 and 34-35 again. Slowly. Make sure you see Jesus' explanation for this. See it with the Supernatural Spiritual Eyes and Mind God has given you as one of His Saints. This is a crucial matter.

Oh, in case you are not aware of those being IN you, look at the 3rd fundamental Truth that follows.

trichotomies – *tri* means 3. In the diagrams in this book picturing God's structure of Himself and the way He created mankind to be, we will see several revelations of God's plan for the ages. After knowing about *revelation* and *parables,* these *trichotomies* will come alive. The truth about how Truth is known to Saints is wrapped up in the diagram picturing the *trichotomy of a Saint.* Yet, the truth about how Saints can read and study the Word of God, and miss God, is in the same trichotomy (every error or false idea comes from the carnal mind in a Saint: Romans 8:6-7). It is a huge revelation.

> For to be carnally minded is death: but to be spiritually minded is life and peace. Because the carnal mind is enmity against God: for it is not subject to the law of God, neither indeed can be.

God speaks of the difference of His Spiritual Mind and the spiritual carnal mind. Saints have both.

The chapter on *What is a Trichotomy?* will give many diagrams of which many have never been seen before. They show the distinct 3-part structural design of each being represented. It does us well to know them and to resort to them to be able to communicate to others what God has designed.

The number 3 is important to God. 3 denotes Divine perfection. Throughout the book we will see God revealing His Divinity through the following list (and others):

3 Lives of God – God the Father (Matthew 23:9), God as the Son (Matthew 1:23; 1 Timothy 2:3,6; 1 Timothy 3:16), God as Holy Spirit (John 14:16; John 17:26 – a hidden parable)

3 Works of God – Creator (Genesis 1:1), Sustainer (Psalm 55:22), Redeemer (Isaiah 47:4)

3 Abilities of Triune God – omniscient (Psalm 147:5), omnipotent (Ephesians 1:19), omnipresent (Jeremiah 23:24)

3 Lives of Saints – the Exchanged Life (Galatians 2:20), the Abiding Life (John 15:5), the Grace Life (1 Corinthians 15:9-10)

3 part structure of everyone – spirit, soul, body (1 Thessalonians 5:23)

3 minds – physical brain (Daniel 2:29), unholy spiritual mind
(1 Corinthians 2:14), Holy Mind of God (1 Corinthians 2:16)

3 beings – God (Hosea 11:9), sinners(Luke 18:13), Saints (Romans 1:7)

3 parts of the soul – mind, emotions, will (Proverbs 2:10)

3 key gifts of Holy Spirit – power, love, sound mind (2 Timothy 1:7)

With these three fundamental premises (Truths) – *revelation, parables, trichotomies* – every Saint is prepared to read the Holy Scriptures and connect with God as no one else can. For in God, and in each Saint,

> …dwell the fullness of the Godhead bodily. And ye are
> complete in him… Colossians 2:9-10

May the entirety of this book be a catalyst for reading and seeing God in every parable/parabolic statement.

chapter 10

What is an Image or Likeness?

And God said, Let us make man in our image,
after our likeness…So God created man in his own image,
in the image of God created he him;
male and female created he them.
Genesis 1:26-27

This is the book of the generations of Adam.
In the day that God created man,
in the likeness of God made he him;
Male and female created he them;
and blessed them, and called their name Adam,
in the day when they were created.
And Adam lived an hundred and thirty years,
and begat a son in his own image.
after his image; and called his name Seth.
Genesis 5:1-3

God introduced two important words in Genesis chapter 1. Two words that give the foundational Truth of the physical and spiritual construct of all individuals. Without knowing completely and understanding correctly no one can See the way God designed earth beings to be of the same three components as He is.

After all other creation was finished, God said *and let us make man in our image, after our likeness.* God spoke through His triune makeup: *let us.* He spoke of *creating* two people, male and female, in His *image* and *likeness.* The two important words: *image* and *likeness.*

A few thousand years later, one is fairly well known. The other has been forgotten (if ever known). And yet it could be the latter is much more definitive, therefore more important, than the first.

However, one of the most erroneous teachings is that ALL individuals are created in the image of God. False. This incorrect teaching leads to all kinds of mistaken ideas, false theology, misleading counseling, and general confusion in the minds (the wrong mind!) of Saints, AND those who have not been Born Again.

I first heard the idea of man being born in the image of Adam way back in 1980 from Adrian Rogers in his "What Every Christian Should Know" series. This was during the very first Church Training class I went to after being Born Again (Sagemont Church, Houston, Texas). Dr. Rogers showed how the Scripture tells us in Genesis that Adam & Eve's kids were begat in Adam's image (Genesis 5:3) and not created in the image of God. All earth beings since then have been begat likewise.

Look at 1 Corinthians 15:42-49,

> So also is the resurrection of the dead. It is sown in corruption; it is raised in incorruption: It is sown in dishonor; it is raised in glory: it is sown in weakness; it is raised in power: It is sown a natural body; it is raised a spiritual body. There is a natural body, and there is a spiritual body. And so it is written, the first man Adam was made a living soul; the last Adam was made a quickening Spirit. Howbeit that was not first which is spiritual, but that which is natural; and afterward that which is spiritual. The first man is of the earth, earthy; the second man is the Lord from heaven. As is the earthy, such are they also that are earthy: and as is the heavenly, such are they also that are heavenly. And as we have borne the image of the earthy, we shall also bear the image of the heavenly.

What a parabolic passage. Heavenly Truth with Heavenly meaning. Truth that frees from erroneous, false thinking.

Today, almost anyone and everyone has heard of *created in the image of God*. Probably 5% actually know what this truthfully is. We actually hear folks from all walks of life claiming to be created in the image of God, and that ALL are born likewise. So let us take a look at this premise from its beginning.

Genesis 1:27 tells us *God created*. Yes, and God is the only One Who can *create*. Remember the definition of create? *To bring something into being that has never before existed. That which only God can do. It does not mean to take something, or two or more somethings, and make something new.* This is a key word the devil has stolen from God's vocabulary. People use the word *create* as if anyone and everybody can create. Not Truth. Not according to God.

Sadly, the Truth about Adam & Eve being the only two individuals who were *created*...by God...is lost upon the multitudes, even Saints. The

Holy Scriptures do not speak of one other person being created by God, as in an individual being brought into being apart from that which has never before existed. Think about it. How has every living earth being been brought into being since Adam & Eve? *Begat*. Begat by a father and mother.

Another sad situation is that the vast majority of Saints today have no clue, idea, or the least thought about there being a distinctly different spiritual construct between a *sinner* and a *Saint*. It could be that 98% think of the difference of a sinner and a Saint as the way one acts…or, should act. And yet when we know the mysterious trichotomy of a sinner and a Saint we can easily see that action has nothing to do with being. Everyone is a being because of a beginning, a birth. Both physically and spiritually. And for Saints, a New Beginning, New Birth.

So as we move along in the book we will discover the distinctive differences and definite details of the makeup of each trichotomy. But let's get what we must know about image and likeness.

The word image is from the Hebrew *tselem* and Greek *eikon*. These words speak of something specific. A reflection. A resemblance. A representative figure. A picture. Photography uses the word image when speaking about the look of someone or something, as well as that which appears on a negative. Except in the use of an x-ray to see the image of the inside of someone or something, this word image refers to an outside appearance. A shape. Neither *tselem* or *eikon* mean an exact duplicate.

Picture the image of a landscape reflected in a pond. There is no look at the inside of whatever is reflected. That is what an image is.

Now think about a likeness. From the Hebrew *demuwth* and Greek *homoioma*. These words speak of that which makes up the design of someone or something, both outside and inside. A similar construct. When looking at this spiritually we can note that God is telling us about the key parts of His design of earth beings after His own construct. That is when we narrow down and we get to the three parts of God and earth beings. A trichotomy of each will show us what the three parts are, where they are located, and we begin to see why God designed and initially created earth beings to be the way we are. Just *like* God. In His *likeness*. It is the recognition of these three parts that can make *likeness* more important than *image*. But for thousands of years the devil has detoured earth beings from thinking about and knowing in detail what this *likeness* is. Again, in chapter 11 we begin to explore these details.

Before we go further, please know we will note the difference in Adam & Eve in the Garden of Eden, Adam & Eve after their sin, all sinners since, a Saint at salvation, and both sinners and Saints in eternity. In the varying dispensations God has designed earth beings to be different depending on the spiritual state of the individual. That is an important fact to make note of.

what is a Trichotomy?

And the very God of peace sanctify you wholly;
and I pray God your whole spirit and soul and body
be preserved blameless unto the coming
of our Lord Jesus Christ.
1 Thessalonians 5:23

Tri means 3. Triune God, 3 manifestations. Tri-cities, 3 cities near each other. Triple, 3 bagger in baseball. Trichotomy, 3 parts to our current physical and spiritual makeup, 1 Thessalonians 5:23 (spirit, soul, body). 3 parts to the soul's likeness (mind, emotions, will). And also 3 parts for the likeness for eternity.

Trichotomy is not a Scriptural word, but identifies the three parts of the image/likeness Scripture mentions spirit/soul/body, our physical and spiritual makeup now. Our mind/emotions/will – spiritual soul now and in eternity. In eternity all will have a spiritual body instead of a physical one. Every being has these two sets of three parts. There are variations of the natural (spiritual) and Supernatural (Spiritual) spirits and souls.

The trichotomies shown diagram *what, how, & why* we are what we are in different manifestations. The same with God. The same with sinners. It is important to recognize how innocency, righteousness, and sinfulness enter in to an accurate look, understanding, and discussion of the trichotomy of individuals. Knowing the variations gives us a picture and explanation of God and earth beings from eternity past to eternity future.

In my book, *The Images of God & Man,* I give some more diagrams, some of which expand on the information about the images given here.

On the following pages are eight basic diagrams that give us a great idea of how God and mankind relate to each other. When we study the 3 parts in detail later in the book, we will find the kind of thinking, feeling, and acting that shows forth from the different individuals. We will also find why Saints sometimes act like Saints and sometimes act like sinners. Yet, once a Saint always a Saint. Thoughts and actions do not make the individual.

GOD in Heaven

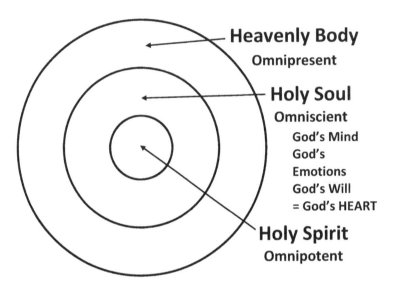

Heavenly Body
Omnipresent

Holy Soul
Omniscient
  God's Mind
  God's
  Emotions
  God's Will
  = God's HEART

Holy Spirit
Omnipotent

This diagram pictures the *Nature* of God. Notice all three parts are with a *capital letter,* recognizing God's Deity. God is God.

God's Omnipotence (all-powerful Holy Spirit) – His Omniscience (all-knowing Holy Soul) – and His Omnipresence (all-present everywhere) are all relative to His image of Deity.

It is important to know that God's Holy Soul houses God's Mind, God's Emotions, and God's Will: the totality of the working of these is God's Heart.

The Lord Jesus Christ on Earth

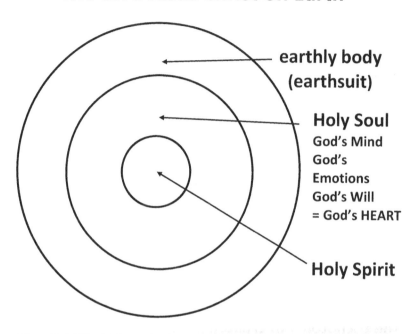

earthly body
(earthsuit)

Holy Soul
God's Mind
God's
Emotions
God's Will
= God's HEART

Holy Spirit

The Trichotomy of the Lord Jesus Christ on Earth pictures the "Nature" of Jesus Christ. Notice His Spirit and His Soul are with a "capital" letter, indicating the Omnipotence (all-powerful Holy Spirit) and Omniscience (all-knowing Holy Soul) in an earthly body (earthsuit)... God in an earthsuit.

This is the IMAGE of GOD...total INNOCENCE and RIGHTEOUSNESS (without sin)... in an earthsuit plus all the inherent qualities of BEING GOD (Love, Joy, Peace, etc., etc., etc.).

Adam & Eve in the Garden of Eden

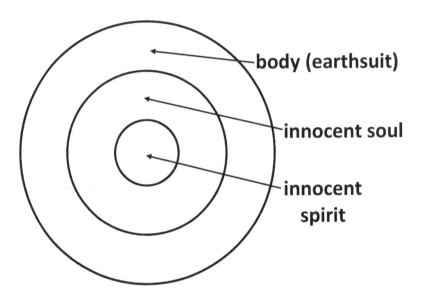

The trichotomy of created man – Adam & Eve in the Garden of Eden.

This diagram pictures the first (man and woman) male and female.

They were created in the image of God, a trichotomy.

Different than God, their spirit and soul were created in innocence. All Scriptures about them in that state testify to that. And their body was earthly and not Heavenly.

Adam & Eve After the "Fall"

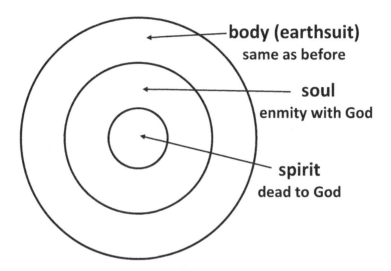

Adam & Eve's *innocence* was taken away, removed, replaced with a *spiritually dead spirit/life* and a *spiritually dead soul* (mind, emotions, will - heart). They were now *sinners.* The *law of sin and death* now ruled them.

Every earthly being is born in this state today (since the Fall) - hence "begat," NOT "created" . . . begat in the Image of Adam.

SINNER

Not a Christian

(called Lost man, Sinner, Unforgiven sinner, Unregenerated man)

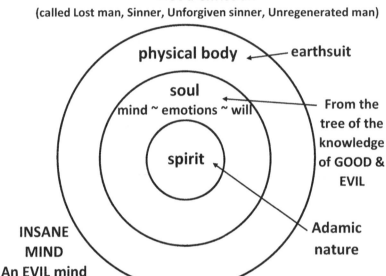

physical body — earthsuit

soul
mind ~ emotions ~ will

spirit

From the
tree of the
knowledge
of GOOD &
EVIL

INSANE
MIND
An EVIL mind

Adamic
nature

This diagram pictures the "Adamic nature" of Unbelievers since the Fall, that which all are physically born with. ALL humans are physically born with this spiritual nature (spirit) and soul. Notice both are with a "small" letter, indicating the absence of Holy Spirit and Christ's Soul.

SINNER
humanism (man is god)
pride (me, not Christ)
self-righteousness
complexity
unbelief
distrust
lies

BORN AGAIN SAINT
The Christian

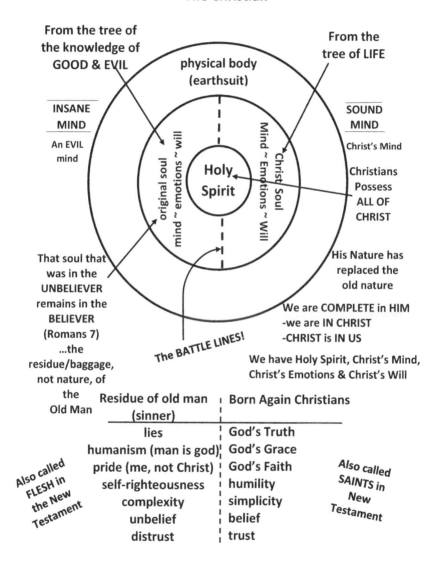

From the tree of
the knowledge of
GOOD & EVIL

From the
tree of LIFE

physical body
(earthsuit)

INSANE
MIND

An EVIL
mind

original soul
mind ~ emotions ~ will

Christ Soul
Mind ~ Emotions ~ Will

Holy
Spirit

SOUND
MIND

Christ's Mind

Christians
Possess
ALL OF
CHRIST

That soul that
was in the
UNBELIEVER
remains in the
BELIEVER
(Romans 7)
...the
residue/baggage,
not nature, of
the
Old Man

His Nature has
replaced the
old nature

We are COMPLETE in HIM
-we are IN CHRIST
-CHRIST is IN US

The BATTLE LINES!

We have Holy Spirit, Christ's Mind,
Christ's Emotions & Christ's Will

Also called
FLESH in
the New
Testament

Also called
SAINTS in
New
Testament

Residue of old man (sinner)	Born Again Christians
lies	God's Truth
humanism (man is god)	God's Grace
pride (me, not Christ)	God's Faith
self-righteousness	humility
complexity	simplicity
unbelief	belief
distrust	trust

Sinners in Hell

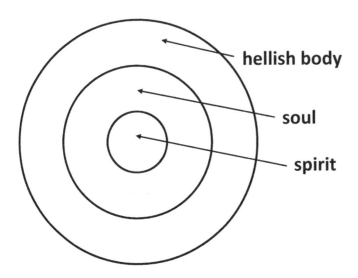

Same soul and spirit as on earth, but new "hellish body".

Interesting – not much is said or written about sinners "living eternally" . . . but they will. In a "hellish body" that Scripture says will burn but never be burnt up.

The entire being of a sinner (hellish body, soul, and spirit) will be tormented eternally.

Saints in Heaven

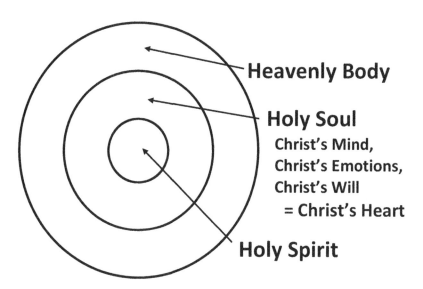

Heavenly Body

Holy Soul
Christ's Mind,
Christ's Emotions,
Christ's Will
    = Christ's Heart

Holy Spirit

The trichotomy of Saints in Heaven...the SAMENESS as GOD and CHRIST. (1 John 3:2; 1 Corinthians 15:49; Philippians 3:21; 2 Corinthians 3:18). BUT...we will NOT be God, or as God totally. God holds the actuality of this mystery from us until we get to Heaven...

This diagram pictures the "Nature" of Saints in Heaven. Notice all are with a "capital" letter, indicating we are in the IMAGE & CHARACTER of GOD completely, but NOT God.

There are many critics of these diagrams. With all kinds of different ideas about spiritual bodies, souls, minds, wills, hearts, etc. Yet I have found none to give an uncomplicated diagram that can stand the test of all of the Holy Scriptures.

And I have yet to have one talk to me about these diagrams of the various trichotomies. They criticize but offer no contrary diagrams. And offer no Scripture that will stand as Truth backed by all the rest of Scripture.

I ask three questions of all who disagree.

1. What was crucified of the *old man*. Virtually all say they agree with Paul saying "I have been crucified…" But what was crucified? We will find out in this book.

2. Was there anything that wasn't crucified? We will find out just what was not crucified in the *sinner/now Saint* at salvation (New Birth).

3. What was created for the crucified sinner to become a Saint? Scripture teaches Saints are a New Creation. We will find out a most crucial Spiritual *part* of God's that was given to all Saints at the New Birth.

Everybody wants to talk about the *old man* and the *new man,* but not address these important questions. Premises that dictate so many aspects of the different dispensations are addressed in this book.

The diagrams of the trichotomies of this chapter denounce much false teaching that leaves Saints powerless (not just by false teachers, who teach there is another way to become a Saint other than by Grace through Faith in the Lord Jesus Christ and His atonement for sin). So many give totally erroneous pictures (diagrams & words) of a mix of Holy Spirit with the human spirit, the nature of Saints as still being sinners, erroneous definitions of Scriptural words (God's words), and the misuse of countless verses. The Truth of all being important to know and understand the Word of God, all because of knowing God's premises.

We will discuss throughout the book just HOW a Saint can miss Truth, believe lies, and argue with one another (when God says we are to be of *one mind,* the *same mind,* and *one accord).* There can be no disagreements of 2 Saints thinking in the Mind of God that is IN every Saint.

When you and I are thinking in the Mind of God, knowing all Spiritual Truth is presented parabolically, and that God has revealed His Heavenly Truth with Heavenly meaning to us…then we must be in agreement.

chapter 12

The Tale of Two Trees

And God said, let the earth bring forth grass,
the herb yielding seed,
and the tree yielding fruit after his kind,
whose seed was in itself, upon the earth: and it was so.
And the earth brought forth grass,
and herb yielding seed after his kind,
and the tree yielding fruit, whose seed was in itself
after his kind: and God saw that it was good.
Genesis 1:11-12

And God said…every tree, in the which is the fruit
of a tree yielding seed; to you it shall be for meat.
Genesis 1:29

And out of the ground made the LORD God to grow every tree
that is pleasant to the sight, and good for food'
the tree of life also in the midst of the garden,
and the tree of knowledge of good and evil.
Genesis 2:9

And the LORD God commanded the man, saying,
Of every tree of the garden thou mayest freely eat:
But of the tree of the knowledge of good and evil,
thou shalt not eat of it: for in the day that thou
eatest thereof thou shalt surely die.
Genesis 2:16-17

In Genesis 1:11-12 God speaks of His creation of trees. In Genesis 1:29 God says every tree will yield seed, *to you it shall be for meat.* But then, in Genesis 2:9 there were two significant trees among the many that were there. God gives them a name, the *tree of life* and the *tree of knowledge of good and evil.* And God put the man He had created in chapter 1 into the garden where these trees were growing. And the LORD God commanded the man, saying, *Of every tree of the garden thou mayest freely eat: But of the tree of the knowledge of good and evil, thou shalt not eat of it: for in the day that thou eatest thereof thou shalt surely die* (Genesis 2:16-17). It was a great parabolic Heavenly Truth with a Heavenly Meaning.

God did not mean they would physically die right then, but would die spiritually. The next time we see these trees mentioned is in Genesis 3:1 where the serpent (parable for the devil) came and talked with Eve, speaking to her innocent spiritual mind, convincing her she would surely not die IF she ate from the forbidden tree. Nothing is said about physical death or spiritual death...just die. The subtle serpent even told Eve directly that if she ate of the forbidden tree she would *know good and evil* (just what God said was the name of the forbidden tree). Eve ate from the forbidden tree and gave to Adam to eat. The rest is history. They both died spiritually at that moment. Losing their innocent spirituality and becoming sinful individuals. This is called the Fall (of Adam & Eve, from innocence).

Many false ideas and many false diagrams (or, descriptions) about Adam & Eve have been made over the years. False ideas and false diagrams yield anyone not knowing Truth. Truth about who Adam & Eve were spiritually created to be. Truth about who Adam & Eve spiritually came to be after their Fall. Spiritual Truth about ALL who have been *begat,* not *created,* since Adam & Eve became sinners. That's every last earth being since Adam & Eve, including you and me at our entrance into this world. And it all came from one of the two trees.

The other tree of importance, the *tree of life,* holds a key to *who* and *what* Saints are like today. It is a Spiritual tree. The tree of Eternal Life. A parabolic representation of the LORD God Himself. Jesus spoke of eating of His body (another parable tied to the *tree of Life).*

> Whoso eateth my flesh, and drinketh my blood, hath eternal life; and I will raise him up at the last day. For my flesh is meat indeed, and my blood is drink indeed. He that eateth my flesh, and drinketh my blood, dwelleth in me, and I in him. John 6:54-56

Incredible, isn't it! Heavenly Truth with Heavenly meaning hidden in a parabolic saying that speaks of the very words we read in Genesis. *Fruit, eat, meat.* Yet how many have never made the connection of those three words in these verses? Why? Parabolic words, parabolic teaching. Known only to those with, and Living in, the Mind of God.

Throughout this book we find references and connections of the two trees and the minds in sinners and Saints. All growing out of the Garden of Eden.

chapter 13

Crucifixion & Creation

Knowing this, that our old man is crucified with him,
that the body of sin might be destroyed,
that henceforth we should not serve sin.
Romans 6:6

Therefore if any man be in Christ,
he is a new creature:
old things are passed away;
behold all things are become new.
2 Corinthians 5:17

I am crucified with Christ:
nevertheless I live; yet not I,
but Christ liveth in me:
and the life which I now live in the flesh
I live by the faith of the Son of God,
who loved me, and gave himself for me.
Galatians 2:20

These two words are important in the understanding of how a sinner becomes a Saint. Two questions must be answered before anyone can know and understand initially Who they are as a Saint. In fact, to know and understand totally Who they are as a Saint.

Q #1 – What is crucified in a sinner at the moment of salvation?
The word crucified is from the Greek *srauroo*. Scripturally it means to be impaled upon a cross. To have *life extinguished and removed* through the process of the crucifixion. *Removed* is an important aspect of this. In a physical crucifixion the physical life is removed, and the spiritual life is removed.

The crucifixion of a sinner at salvation is a spiritual crucifixion. Not a physical one. A sinner is not crucified on a cross physically and spiritually. The sinner is spiritually crucified by Holy Spirit. The earthsuit remains alive, but the old Adamic, sinful, natural spirit is crucified (killed and removed). Understanding this changes a lot of thinking that has been popular and prevalent for years. This is a matter multitudes have wondered about and questioned forever, but no Scriptural answer was pointed out.

So a sinner crucified is left with the earthsuit and the old Adamic, sinful, natural soul. That presents the crucified sinner to be created as a Saint.

Q #2 – What is created in a Saint at the moment of salvation?
In a speed unknown to mankind, Holy Spirit creates in the crucified sinner two parts of the Divine Being. One is Holy Spirit, Who replaces the Adam spirit, as the Life of the Saint. The other is Holy Soul, a new and 2nd soul in a Saint.

Holy Spirit and Holy Soul are the new creation of a Saint. The Divine Life and Divine Living in the old earthsuit of the individual. Very few Saints are ever taught about what is created at salvation, all the while quoting 2nd Corinthians 5:17 about being a new creation, and all the while never coming to an understanding of just what that is. In essence, never coming to a complete understanding of Who they are as a Saint.

If we don't know Who we are (the Divine creation of God destined for Eternal Life with Him), and all that is, then how can we enjoy Life as a Christian? How can we enjoy the Life and Presence of God IN us? His freedom from sin?

No wonder a multitude of Saints go around thinking God is "out to get them" for doing wrong, but never think of His Grace in their Lives, of what their truthful Spiritual Life is. We will discover the real Life of a Saint Spiritually…that which is most important to God. And should be for us Saints.

Before we leave this chapter, let's take a look at something well worth noticing and knowing. The phrase *body of sin (soma tou hamartia)* in Romans 6:6. Here we see *body,* as mentioned back in chapter 7 on page 33 (definition of *body*) the Greek *soma,* can have meanings in Scripture other than to identify an earth being's earthsuit. This is one of them. It is somewhat a parabolic reference to the entity that encapsulates sin *(hamartia)* in a sinner.

In another verse, Romans 6:12, *soma* refers to the *body* as the earthsuit of an earth being (mortal body – *thnetos soma)*. Keeping track of the Greek words along with the different uses gives us God's clear, uncomplicated, and not confusing picture of sin and where it comes from in a Saint. If anyone attributes *body* in Romans 6:6 with *soma* as in an *earthsuit*, then the crucifixion of the *body of sin,* destroyed, leads to an immediate confusion since the earthsuit is still around.

As we continue to progress through the book, we will find more details about this salvation and both of the creations. For now, know and remember: *no longer a sinner, instantly a Saint with no sin.* A parabolic Truth. That is a big discussion later.

chapter 14

What is a Spiritual Soul?

Now I beseech you, brethren,
by the name of our Lord Jesus Christ,
that ye all speak the same thing,
and that there be no divisions among you;
but that ye be perfectly joined together
in the same mind and in the same judgment.
1 Corinthians 1:10

This I say therefore, and testify in the Lord,
that ye henceforth walk not as other Gentiles walk,
in the vanity of their mind,
Having understanding darkened,
being alienated from the life of God
through the ignorance that is in them,
because of the blindness of their heart:
Who being past feeling have given themselves
over unto lasciviousness, to work all uncleanness with greediness.
But ye have not so learned Christ.
Ephesians 4:17-20

There is a spiritual entity inside every person that has three spiritual parts: spiritual mind, spiritual emotions, and spiritual will-decider-commitment. The sum of the working of these three is the spiritual heart. All of these are inside what Scripture refers to as the *soul*. These are completely separate from the physical *soma*.

A lot of people attribute different thoughts, emotions, and actions to the spirit. This includes numerous Saints referring to Holy Spirit as having those capacities. It is the soul where those activities emanate from.

Without the knowledge of the soul's parts and activity, and attributing the work of the soul to the spirit, the ability for a Saint to decide which soul we will function out of is greatly diminished, if not entirely so. For many there is no thought of being able to decide, or why there is a decision.

Solomon wrote some pointed words in Proverbs 19:20-21,

Hear counsel, and receive instruction, that thou mayest be wise in they latter end. There are many devices in a man's heart; nevertheless the counsel of the LORD, that shall stand.

And in Proverbs 12:15,

The way of a fool is right in his own eyes: but he that hearkeneth unto counsel is wise.

And in Proverbs 11:14,

Where no counsel is, the people fall…

Hosea spoke in Hosea 4:6, *My people are destroyed for lack of knowledge.* Hosea was one of God's prophets, and here he was prophesying (speaking God's Truth) to the people of the Northern Kingdom (Israel). He was giving the Lord's controversy with Israel. It is extremely interesting he was making his declarations at the very same time Solomon was doing so in Judah, in the Southern Kingdom. Both prophets spoke of the dire results of not knowing or rejecting God's knowledge and wisdom.

Without a shadow of any doubt, we must have the wise counsel of the parabolic Holy Scriptures.

Scripture is full of references to the soul and its activity. What Scripture does not identify most of the time is *which* soul…carnal or Holy. With not much teaching about Saints having a Holy Soul, or even what any soul is, Saints are left with inadequate information to know and understand a lot of why we think like we think and do what we do. This is truth in all instances, whether righteous or unholy.

Our text verses gave reference to these. It is important to know there are two different spiritual souls. Some of this I mentioned under *What is a Parable?* In the next section we will look at WHY there are two different souls.

Let it be known from the start that every Saint (a Born Again, New Creation individual) possesses *two souls.* This was God's design from the beginning. It is an important aspect of Life as a Saint while still on earth. And it is an important aspect of *what* of a Saint goes to Heaven upon the physical death on earth. Apart from having *two souls* there is no explanation for a lot of things Scripture speaks of concerning the dilemma Paul mentions in Romans 6-8 and the Life Paul mentions in Galatians 2:20.

And there are many other verses of the Holy Scriptures that speak of *the soul* or *our soul,* and without the knowledge of a Saint having *two souls* and the difference of *one soul from another* there is no understanding of what God is really telling us. This is part of the parabolic teaching of the Holy Scriptures.

Without knowing, understanding, believing, and receiving the Truth about...

1. parables, and the Scriptural definition of parables/parabolic teaching
2. the entirety of Spiritual Truth in Scripture is written in parables or parabolic wording

...no Saint KNOWS God's Words to His people. Scripture tells us that.

We can often think we know, but we often have been deceived by the carnal mind.

- example: When God says over & over & over all Saints are to be of one Mind, in one accord...it is unacceptable to have disagreements and arguments.
  It is unacceptable to take votes in a gathering and function where any majority rules. Even the decision to have different percentages of majorities on different votes is an affront to God.
- Majority is not in God's vocabulary. Vote is not even in God's vocabulary. Both have led to more disunity and deviation from the Mind of God than most anything in any gathering/assembly.
- Unanimity only comes from the Mind of God

Knowing, understanding, believing, and receiving Truth only comes in the Mind of God.

There are several foundational fundamental premises in Scripture that unlock and reveal Truth to a Saint. In fact, it is only by revelation from God that Truth can be known. All of this takes place in the Holy Soul.

71

chapter 15

Two Souls – a hidden mystery

A double-minded man is unstable in all his ways.
James 1:8

Mysteries with God are not something new. All Spiritual Truth is a mystery until God has revealed it. A read through the Holy Scriptures shows several incredible mysteries that were revealed at a time in history when God deemed it time. So now we get to the crux of the trichotomy of a Saint. Two spiritual souls, two spiritual minds. Along with a physical brain. Sorting out the things in life depend on knowing about these three minds and how they are to fit into our daily functions, both physically and spiritually.

The Truth about a Saint having two spiritual souls (referred to as 2 souls henceforth) has been hidden from most in Christianity for many, many years. And yet it holds Truth that dramatically empowers each and every Saint who knows and Lives the Life of Holy Spirit within..

In the first chapter of James we are given a clear picture of the 2 souls. See the real issue of these 2 souls in five verses:

> If any of you lack wisdom, let him ask of God, that giveth
> to all men liberally, and upbraideth not; and it shall be
> given him. But let him ask in faith, nothing wavering, For
> he that wavereth is like a wave of the sea driven with the
> wind and tossed. For let not that man think that he shall
> receive any thing of the Lord. A double-minded man is
> unstable in all his ways. James 1:4-8

A *double-minded man.* On the surface, that could be taken to think of someone thinking one way one minute, and another way another minute. With the same mind. The key is the Greek *dipsuchos.* From *dis,* twice, and *psuche,* soul or mind. When we know the *mind* is in the *soul,* the Heavenly Truth stands out: *twice-souled.* 2 souls.

How is this important? *Twice-souled,* 2 souls, 2 minds. The souls and minds being diametrically opposed to each other.

The 2 souls are mentioned many times throughout the post-Pentecost scriptures. Solidifying the Truth about their place in the Life of a Saint.

There are three passages that are a parabolic testimony revealing the presence of the 2 souls, the function of the 2 souls, and the powerful difference of the 2 souls.

- *But the natural man receiveth not the things of the Spirit of God: for they are foolishness unto him: neither can he know them, because they are spiritually discerned.* 1 Corinthians 2:14

- *But he that is spiritual judgeth all things, yet he himself is judged of no man. For who hath known the mind of the Lord, that he may instruct him? But we have the mind of Christ.* 1 Corinthians 2:15-16

- *For to be carnally minded is death: but to be spiritually minded is life and peace. Because the carnal mind is enmity against God: for it is not subject to the law of God, neither indeed can be.* Romans 8:6-7

Think about 1 Corinthians 2:14. The natural man is speaking of being in the state of that as a sinner. Spiritually separated from God, dead in trespasses and sins. The mind of a natural man/sinner in the only soul he has is one that cannot receive the things of the Spirit of God, they are foolishness to him, and cannot know them because they are spiritually discerned. This is a profound declaration of the impotence of the natural mind.

How often do we stop to think of the impact in a sinner living in a spiritual world as well as the physical world? Living in both spiritually blinded affects everything in both worlds of a sinner. In fact, we have to acknowledge this ignorance and blindness. That is the ignorance and blindness to spiritual things of the natural mind. This impacts how Saints should interact with sinners.

The old deceitful devil brings all sorts of distortions that lead the sinner to think they know Truth. When they can't. The enemy gives humanistic thinking and interpretations to the natural mind yielding a blind, religious individual. Think of all the blindness of the multitudes whom Jesus and the disciples shared Truth with to no avail. And it is still the same today.

Now think on 1 Corinthians 2:15-16. This is a testimony of one who is a Saint. A Saint is Spiritual, Spiritually alive in Christ. Holy Spirit and Holy Soul indwelling. God verifies this with the words, *But we have the mind of Christ.* God's Holy Mind is in Holy Soul.

Then look at Romans 8:6-7. God brings a new word into the discussion. *Carnal.* This word in the New Testament speaks of the *natural mind* that is a residue mind in each Saint from the old, sinner man. The same mind of a sinner, but *the carnal mind* is what God calls that mind in a Saint. Here God gives more information: death (spiritual, in the carnal mind that is alienated from God's Mind), life and peace (in the Mind of God), enmity (in the carnal mind that has hatred, hostility, and animosity against God), and the carnal mind is *not subject to the law of God, neither indeed can be.*

- Saints do have the carnal mind from when a sinner man.

What we will find in the rest of the book is the vast difference in these 2 minds in the 2 souls and how they enter into the day to day activities of a Saint.

Before we go any further, let us think of how this mystery has prevailed. If a Saint doesn't know about, or hasn't accepted, that all Saints have 2 souls, then they will have a difficult time knowing, understanding, believing, and receiving the Holy Scriptures. God says so.

A very interesting and important point to know: this natural/carnal mind can think and know *religious* thoughts that appear to be God's Truth, but are nothing more than a deception and detour away from the Truth of God. Anyone, including a sinner, can know and discuss the *words* of the Holy Scriptures, but only The Mind of God knows the *Heavenly Truths* of the Holy Scriptures. When we speak, "The Scripture says…" we must be speaking Heavenly Truth.

How are ALL the Holy Scriptures received, known, and understood? God tells us how.

- Saints do have The Mind of Christ (God).

Let's think about this issue of a Saint not knowing we possess the actual Spiritual Holy Mind of God. If we have something, but we do not know that we have it, how often do we use it? Example: we have an account in our name at our bank with $1,000,000 in it. But we do not know we have that account. We do not have any knowledge of the account existing. How much of the $1,000,000 have we used? Therefore, if we have two souls (with all the parts to each soul), but we do not know we have the two, how often do we use each one? The answer to all these questions is: we don't use what we don't know we have.

This leaves two possibilities that should also be considered. How many Saints never use The Mind of Christ in them? As such, there can be no knowledge (or, use) of real Spiritual Truth. Is that interesting, or what? Perhaps alarming to many. Another is the possibility there are many people who consider themselves to be Christians, but are not. We will look more in detail at that later in the book.

One thing for sure, God has revealed Spiritual Truth. It is revealed to those who have been given the Holy Soul of God with The Mind of God. Heavenly Truth with Heavenly meaning. And no Heavenly Truth is revealed to the natural or carnal mind. Just reading the words, or memorizing and quoting them, from the printed pages of whatever bible we have does not correlate to knowing Divine Heavenly Truth..

Very few individuals are aware of a Saint having 2 souls. In fact, this is usually why there is so much confusion with people who think someone became a Christian, but the New Saint *doesn't always act like it.* People think the convert has not really become a Christian (ever notice they don't think the same thing about someone they have known for a long time who acts the same as the new convert?). This is really sad thinking to start with. Christianity has never been about how one *acts,* but what one's *birth* is. This is also why there is so much confusion with Saints who are befuddled at why they think some of the things they think, and do some of the things they do…when they are not supposed to think and act that way as Saints. Now remember, Scripture tells us that with God there is no confusion.

Every individual, earth being, is originally born a *physical* being and a *spiritual* being. One thing to always keep in mind, it is the *spiritual* being that will live eternally; sinners in hell, Saints in Heaven.

God determined that the consequence of Adam's sin would be passed down physically (death of earthsuit) and spiritually (being a sinner separated from God) to every generation of earth beings.

> Wherefore, as by one man sin entered into the world, and death by sin; and so death passed upon all men, for that all have sinned: For until the law sin was in the world: but sin is not imputed when there is no law, Nevertheless death reigned from Adam to Moses, even over them that had not sinned after the similitude of Adam's transgression, who is the figure of him that was to come…Therefore as

by the offence of one judgment came upon all men to condemnation...For as by one man's disobedience many were made sinners. Romans 5:12-14, 18, 19

As it is written, There is none righteous, no not one: there is none that understandeth, there is none that seeketh after God. Romans 3:10-11

All have sinned, and come short of the glory of God. Romans 3:23

For since by man came death...For as in Adam all die...There are celestial bodies, and bodies terrestrial...So also is the resurrection of the dead. It is sown in corruption...It is sown in dishonor...It is sown in weakness...It is sown a natural body...The first man is of the earth, earthy...As is the earthy, such are they also that are earthy...And as we have borne the image of the earthy...Now this I say , brethren, that flesh and blood cannot inherit the kingdom of God; neither doth corruption inherit incorruption. 1 Corinthians 15:21, 22, 40, 42, 43, 44, 47, 48, 49, 50

This is the book of the generations of Adam. In the day that God created man, in the likeness of God made he him...And Adam lived an hundred and thirty years, and begat a son in his own likeness, after his image; and called his name Seth: And the days of Adam after he had begotten Seth were eight hundred years: and he begat sons and daughters. And all the days that Adam lived were nine hundred and thirty years: and he died. Genesis 5:1, 3-5

Adam & Eve still had the physical body they were created with. But their *innocent* spirit and soul were changed to a *sinful* spirit and *sinful* soul. This sinful soul is called the *natural* soul which houses the natural mind-emotions-will. The sum of the actions of these three equaling the *natural* heart of sinners. All of which is enmity with God. God has made clear that all are first born *in Adam,* sinners, and cannot inherit the kingdom of God.

But what about when a sinner becomes a Saint? We can thank God great Spiritual changes occur. The old sinful spirit is crucified and removed. However, the sinful soul is left (I refer to it as the *residue* soul). The diagram on p. 58 shows the makeup of a sinner with 1 spiritual soul, and the diagram on p. 59 shows the makeup of a Saint having two spiritual souls. There is also further explanation on the pages following the diagrams.

This dramatic change occurs in the spiritual being. The physical body (earthsuit) remains the same. Just as it did in the dramatic spiritual change of Adam & Eve. God tells us there will be a dramatic change from the earthsuit to an eternal suit at the physical death. All of this is hidden to sinners in the wonderful Spiritual parables in all of Scripture. God's explanation has told us that His parabolic teaching is unrecognizable and impossible to be understood by the natural man. But all is to be seen, heard, and understood by those with the 2nd Soul, the Holy Soul from the New Creation.

> But the natural man receiveth not the things of the Spirit of God: for they are foolishness to him: neither can he know them, because they are spiritually discerned. 1 Corinthians 2:14

> But if our gospel be hid, it is hid to them that are lost: In whom the god of this world hath blinded the minds of them which believe not, lest the light of the glorious gospel of Christ, who is the image of God, should shine unto them. 2 Corinthians 4:3-4

Let's look again at the important verses in Matthew ch. 13 (first given on pgs 18-19).

> The same day went Jesus out of the house, and sat by the sea side. And great multitudes were gathered together unto him, so that he went into a ship, and sat; and the whole multitude stood on the shore. And he spake many things unto them in parables, saying, Behold, a sower went forth

77

to sow; And when he sowed, some seeds fell by the way side, and the fowls came and devoured them up: Some fell on stony places, where they had not much earth: and forthwith they sprung up, because they had no deepness of earth: And when the sun was up, they were scorched: and because they had no root, they withered away. And some fell among thorns; and the thorns sprung up, and choked them: But other fell into good ground, and brought forth fruit, some an hundredfold, some sixtyfold, some thirtyfold. Who hath ears to hear, let him hear.
Matthew 13:1-9

This is the start of some fascinating revelation from God about parables and souls. Let us continue and see as God's explanation begins:

And the disciples came, and said unto him, Why speakest thou unto them in parables? He answered and said unto them, Because it is given unto you to know the mysteries of the kingdom of heaven, but unto them it is not given. For whosoever hath, to him shall be given, and he shall have more abundance: but whosoever hath not, from him shall be taken away even that he hath. Therefore speak I to them in parables: because seeing they see not; and hearing they hear not, neither do they understand. And in them is fulfilled the prophecy of Esaias, which saith, By hearing ye shall hear, and shall not understand; and seeing ye shall see, and not perceive: For this people's heart is waxed gross, and their ears are dull of hearing, and their eyes they have closed; lest at any time they should see with their eyes and hear with their ears, and should understand with their heart, and should be converted, and I should heal them. But blessed are your eyes, for they see: any your ears, for they hear. For verily I say unto you, That many prophets and righteous men have desired to see those things which ye see, and have not seen them: and to hear those things which ye hear, and have not heard them.
Matthew 13:10-17

Sometimes there are parables within the overall parable. As an example: Matthew 13:11-12, 16. This is Jesus speaking to His disciples of when Saints post-Pentecost will have His Holy Soul with His Holy Mind *as if they have them!* Even though they did not possess either just yet. The parable within the parable.

Let's stop and review some key points and their impact.

- Spiritual mysteries cannot be understood in the natural or carnal minds.
- Saints can know Scriptural mysteries via Holy Soul with the Mind of God and God's revelation of the mysteries.
- Sinners in the unholy soul with the unholy, natural mind cannot ever know any Scriptural Spiritual mysteries.
- A Scriptural parable is Heavenly Truth with Heavenly meaning, sometimes using an earthly illustration (as in Matthew 13), but not always…in fact, these occur very few times in comparison to when no earthly illustration is given.
- Jesus speaks in terms of his closest disciples HAVING the Eyes, Ears, and Mind to be given the capacity to See, Hear, and Understand. But, they did not have Holy Soul just yet. WHY is this spoken as such? It is another great parabolic statement giving Truth that can only be known and understood in the Mind of God. It is Holy Spirit giving Matthew a recollection 35+ years later of Jesus speaking when the disciples did not see, hear, and understand in their natural mind. But Matthew did possess the Mind of God post-Pentecost at the time of his writing.

Where does all thinking go on? Why did God design Saints to have 2 spiritual souls? Why do Saints at times think the things we think that are not from God? Or, think things we know are not from God? Why do we do the things we do that we know not from God? But, also, think and do things we know ARE of God? That is what we will look into in chapter 16, Why Two Souls?

Why Two Souls?

But the natural man receiveth not the things
of the Spirit of God.: for they are foolishness
unto him: neither can he know them,
because they are spiritually discerned...
But we have the mind of Christ.
1 Corinthians 2:14, 16

Now if I do that I would not,
it is no more I that do it,
but sin that dwelleth in me.
I find then a law, that,
when I would do good,
evil is present with me.
For I delight in the law of God
after the inward man:
But I see another law in my members,
warring against the law of my mind,
and bringing me into captivity
to the law of sin which is in my members.
O wretched man that I am!
Who shall deliver me from the body of this death?
I thank God through Jesus Christ our Lord.
So then with the mind I myself serve the law of God;
but with the flesh the law of sin.
Romans 7:20-25

If a Saint doesn't know about, or hasn't accepted, that all Saints have 2 spiritual souls/2 spiritual minds, then they will have a difficult time knowing, understanding, believing, and receiving Truth in the Spiritual Holy Scriptures. This happens only because of functioning in the carnal mind when a Saint does not know or acknowledge having the Holy Soul & Mind of God. God says so.

For to be carnally minded is death: but to be spiritually
minded is life and peace. Because the carnal mind is enmity

against God: for it is not subject to the laws of God, neither indeed can be. Romans 8:6-7

Living in the carnal mind is a tragic missing out on all the Holy Soul and Holy Mind bring to each Saint.

Think of the deception of the devil. A Saint cannot be the new Spiritual creation without both Holy Spirit and Holy Soul. Yet, Saints declare they have Holy Spirit but do not have God's Holy Mind. Impossible. Saints deceived and detoured from Truth.

Let's revisit a couple of reasons God leaves the *natural mind* of the *natural man* (called *carnal mind* at the new creation) IN Saints at salvation. Keep handy the diagrams of the trichotomies of Jesus on earth and a Saint on earth. These point clearly to God's design and intentions.

First and foremost, compare what a Saint with only Holy Soul would look like compared to Jesus on earth. The exact same, correct? This could not be. Otherwise, we would be as we *will be* in Heaven. So for the time remaining on earth after becoming a new creation, God leaves the unholy soul intact. Later to be removed at the physical death.

This is important. Saints on earth could not have the exact same trichotomy as Jesus did when He walked the earth. We do have Holy Spirit and Holy Soul which is the forerunner of our Eternal trichotomy when we die physically. What does God have to give His Saints at the physical death? A Heavensuit. (see diagram on p. 60) And Saints will only have 1 soul in Heaven...Holy Soul.

Secondly, God has left the unholy soul so we would be totally and completely dependent on Him for His Life in our remaining days on earth. Dependent on His Life for all things pertaining to the Spiritual realm. It is known as *the saving Life of Christ*. Holy Spirit is our Spiritual Life. He desires to be allowed to Live Spiritually through a Saint's earthsuit. This is another mystery to many, but once the revelation comes, great freedom and power is experienced by a Saint.

It is impossible for a Saint to Live Life as a Saint through the unholy soul. There are moments when the unholy soul rears its ugly head and makes itself known through a Saint, but this is not God's plan for His Saints.

Think about it. Holy Spirit Life. Holy Soul (Mind, Emotions, Will = Holy Heart). Now that is what the Spiritual in Christianity is all about. 100% God, 0% us. Supernaturally Spiritually alive. Thinking God's thoughts at all times, feeling as God feels at all times, choosing/making decisions/taking actions as God does at all times. The Heart of God showing Himself strong in the earthsuit of a Saint.

All Saints have been given the Supernatural Spiritual Mind of God at the New Birth/New Creation. With God's Mind He can reveal absolute Spiritual Truth to each and every Saint. Saints do not learn Truth. Truth is revealed to Saints. Reading the Holy Scriptures gives God an opportunity to take His Words of Life and reveal them to a Saint at God's appointed time. Amazing revelations can come each and every day! They do! Truth never before seen in the carnal mind.

Experiencing emotional control and expression is available to each and every Saint. Think about that. Think about the peaceful, calm, worry-free, anxiety-free, fear-free Life. How does that sound compared to those demonic-inspired thoughts, emotions, and decisions that have haunted you all your life? From your carnal mind.

Reading verses like John 14:27,

> Peace I leave with you, my peace I give unto you: not as the world giveth, give I unto you. Let not your heart be troubled, neither let it be afraid.

God's Life of Peace becomes ours in the Mind and Emotions of God.

Verses like Philippians 4:6-9 come bounding off the page.

> Be careful *(worried/anxious)* for nothing: but in every thing by prayer *(communion with God)* and supplication with thanksgiving let your requests be made known to God. And the peace of God, which passeth all understanding, shall keep your hearts and minds through Christ Jesus. Finally, brethren, whatsoever things are true, whatsoever things are honest, whatsoever things are just, whatsoever things are pure, whatsoever things are lovely, whatsoever things are of good report; if there be any virtue, and if there be any praise, think on these things. Those things, which ye have both learned, and received, and hear, and see in me, do: and the God of peace shall be with you.

Where does all this thinking, feeling, and doing come from? The God of Peace. God's Life in a Saint's earthsuit. God doing all these things. Not us. Our old man was crucified at salvation. Believe it. God's Life becomes ours in the Mind, Emotions, and Chooser (Will) of God in our earthsuit.

So much in Christianity is centered around the Two Souls. Knowing this gives a Saint the Vision to See things that anyone not knowing of or possessing the Mind of God is not privileged to enjoy His Life.

Sadly, very little teaching/preaching is given to there being 2 spiritual Souls, and that Saints have both. Therefore, very few teachers/preachers even touch the Scriptural Truth about why Saints think/feel/decide/do in an ungodly way one minute, then think/feel/decide/do in a godly way the next minute. They give no information, no reason, no help in getting a handle on WHY this is, and HOW to overcome the ungodly.

Oh, Victory in Jesus that every Saint loves to sing about is only available and Livable IN the Holy Soul. Let me repeat, Christianity has never been about how one *acts,* but what one's *birth* is. This is also why there is so much confusion with Saints who are befuddled at why they think some of the things they think, and do some of the things they do...when they are not supposed to think and act that way as Saints.

When a sinner becomes a Saint, we can thank God great Spiritual changes occur. These dramatic changes occur in the spiritual being. The physical body (earthsuit) remains the same. Just as it did in the dramatic spiritual change of Adam & Eve. God tells us there will be a dramatic change from the earthsuit to an Eternal heavensuit for Saints at the physical death. All of this is hidden to sinners (even Saints in the carnal mind) in the wonderful Spiritual parables in all of Scripture. But all is to be seen, heard, and understood by those with the 2nd Soul, the Holy Soul from the New Creation.

A quick recap will remind us of key points to always remember:

- Mysteries are for Saints via Holy Soul with the Mind of God.
- Mysteries are not for sinners with the unholy soul with the unholy, natural mind.
- Sometimes there are parables within the overall parable. As an example: Matthew 13:11-12, 16.
- A Scriptural parable is Heavenly Truth with Heavenly meaning, sometimes using an earthly illustration (as in this case), but not always...in fact, few times in comparison to when no earthly illustration is given.
- Jesus speaks in terms of his closest disciples HAVING the eyes, ears, and mind to be given the capacity to see, hear, and

understand. But, they did not have Holy Soul just yet. WHY is this spoken as such? It is Holy Spirit giving Matthew a recollection 30-35 years later of Jesus speaking when the disciples did not see, hear, and understand in their natural mind. But Matthew did possess the Mind of God post-Pentecost which includes the time of his writing.

God designed Saints to have 2 souls. A remarkable design we must acknowledge if we stop and think through all it means and involves. A Saint not knowing or acknowledging the possession of God's Holy Soul with His Holy Mind leaves the Saint still functioning in the residue carnal mind left over from the sinner days.

God has given His Saints His Holy Spirit and His Holy Soul to experience His Holiness and Righteousness. But He left as a residue the old, unholy, carnal soul where we would not be as Jesus was when He walked this terra firma…and that we would be dependent upon Him for our remaining days on earth.

His design for Saints now has given us all we ever will be in eternity except a new suit…a Heavensuit. Oh, what a day that will be, when we step up to Heaven with our Holy Spirit and our Holy Soul and our Heavensuit. *Just as He is, but never Him.* Still a mystery.

chapter 17

From Beginning to Now

In the beginning God created
the heaven and the earth...
Genesis 1:1

We then, as workers together with him, beseech you
also that ye receive not the grace of God in vain.
For he saith, I have heard thee in a time accepted,
and in the day of salvation have I succored thee:
behold, now is the accepted time;
behold, now is the day of salvation.
2 Corinthians 6:1-2

Everything in existence points toward Eternity. Every day before is a setting of the stage for Life forever. For Saints that is an Eternity with God. Creation, the Garden of Eden, and creation of male & female started God's process of building toward forever and forever. Salvation opens the door to that Eternity with God.

The different dispensations have been a time of God moving toward what we call the *end of time.*

> And this gospel of the kingdom shall be preached in all the world for a witness unto all nations; and then shall the end come. Matthew 24:14

> Heaven and earth shall pass away: but my words shall not pass away. But of that day and that hour knoweth no man, no not the angels which are in heaven, neither the Son, but the Father. Mark 13:31-32
> But the day of the Lord will come as a thief in the night; in the which the heavens shall pass away with a great voice and the elements shall melt with fervent heat, the earth also and the works that are therein shall be burned up. 2 Peter 3:10

All the days and years since creation have been a part of the plan of God. We are living in what many call the *last dispensation* before the coming of the Lord, the new earth, the new Jerusalem (Eternity). And in this dispensation, God has designed His people to be something Scripture has never before shown. A Spiritual person with two souls.

How and why are we at this stage of time? Let us think back from creation and walk through the ages in quick fashion. Let us look at some different manifestations of God and us.

a. God and Adam & Eve

Scripture speaks of man being *created in the image of God*. Yet how many ever think about what that really means?

> And God said, Let us make man in our image, after our likeness...So God created man in his own image, in the image of God created he him; male and female created he them. Genesis 1:26-27

We have seen there are two references in this *creation* that most everyone never takes the time to look up the original Hebrew words or the context of all Scripture: *image* and *likeness*. And both are important to understand the *spiritual being* of mankind.

From the beginning, God and man have been two different spiritual beings. God is 100% Holy. Adam & Eve were created 100% innocent, not Holy. Therefore the *Holy* and the *innocent* were different for the obvious reasons. God has never been, and never will/could be a *man*. Likewise, *man* was not created to be God, or be a god. And never would be. Take another look at the diagrams on pages 54 & 56.

Then Adam & Eve *sinned*, hence their *Fall* from innocence. Their spiritual soul was immediately *of sin* (spiritual separation from God). All mankind since have been *begat sinners with a spirit of sin and a soul of sin*. None have been *created*. There is not one mention in the Holy Scriptures since Adam & Eve sinned of *a man* being *created*. All have been *begat*.

Here is another proof that no *man* since Adam & Eve has been *created*...since none are born *innocent*. All are born *sinners*, the consequence put upon mankind by God since the *Fall*. *Man* disappeared at the Fall. *Sinner man* is everyone born since. *Innocence* from the creation disappeared.

86

b. a sinner

> As it is written, There is none righteous, no, not one:
> Romans 3:10
> For all have sinned, and come short of the glory of God.
> Romans 3:23
> But God commendeth his love toward us, in that, while
> we were yet sinners, Christ died for us. Romans 5:8

Take a look again at the diagram of a sinner on page 58. A drastic change from the innocence of Adam & Eve in the Garden of Eden. Same ole physical earthsuit. But now an unholy spirit and unholy soul. Both are a consequence of Adam & Eve's separation from God by separating themselves from belief, trust, and dependence on God…and eating of the fruit (life) of the forbidden tree.

Adam & Eve partook of the life of the devil. That was the fruit of the forbidden tree. That life knows *good* and *evil*. Neither of which are of the righteousness of God. Adam & Eve chose a life of separation from God. They instantaneously knew it!

> And the eyes of them both were opened, and they knew
> they were naked; and they sewed fig leaves together, and
> made themselves aprons. And they heard the voice of the
> LORD God walking in the garden in the cool of the day:
> and Adam and his wife hid themselves from the presence
> of the LORD God amongst the trees of the garden.
> Genesis 3:7-8

What a parabolic passage! This was not a simple opening of their mind to understand some new things, but to partake of the forbidden life and be changed from innocent spiritual fellowship with God to spiritual separation from God. That is sin.

Adam & Eve did not have to be told their fellowship was damaged. They didn't have to have some preacher put them down for their *sin*. They didn't have to hear some gossiping brothers and sisters whisper to one another about their *sin*. They knew immediately.

But have you noticed God didn't bring down fire and brimstone on them? From v. 13 and their excuses before God, God turned and cursed the serpent. Yes, God did bring some consequences on Adam & Eve, but the Scriptures never say God cursed them, or any offspring.

Sinners today do not need to be told of their sin. Their unholy soul reminds them. They know it and feel it

c. a Saint

When a sinner is Born Again, it is both interesting and incredible that the new creation consists of two new spiritual parts: a Holy Spirit and a Holy Soul. This makes the new Saint *as* God *is* Spiritually.

However each Saint has 2 souls. A residue carnal soul from the time of being a sinner. The Holy Soul is newly created at salvation. All spiritual battles in a Saint occur between these 2 souls. A Saint only has 1 Spirit, Holy Spirit. There can be no battles in the Holy Spirit or Holy Soul. There can be some physical battles in the Saint's earthsuit. But all spiritual battles in a Saint occur *between* these 2 souls. This cannot be emphasized too much.

Many erroneous, thereby false, thoughts, fears, definitions and statements are made by not being aware of where the battles are from. We hear folks say all the time, *I am restless in my spirit.* Impossible for a Saint. Or, *There is a battle going on in my* spirit. Impossible for a Saint. *My spirit is weak,* or *I am feeling down in my spirit.* Impossible for a Saint. All of these are impossible in Holy Spirit, the only Spirit of a Saint.

Stop and think of all the different ways we can be deceived. Being acutely aware of where the battle is taking place gives way to a quick resolution to the battle. Get out of the unholy soul and into Holy Soul.

Saint or Saints are mentioned 61 times in the New Testament. God's name for His kids. Holy, Righteous, Sinless. Three of the most beautiful identities of every Saint. One of the greatest proofs that a Saint cannot *sin* (as the Scriptures call it) is that a Saint can never be spiritually separated from God!

> Let your conversation be without covetousness; and be content with such things as ye have: for he hath said, I will never leave thee, nor forsake thee. Hebrews 13:5

> But ye are not in the flesh, but in the Spirit, if so be that the Spirit of God dwell in you. Now if any man have not the Spirit of Christ, he is none of his. Romans 8:9

What a marvelous Truth. God in us forever from the moment of salvation. And He will never leave us. The Spiritual Birth from above is solid proof of this issue. Saints can never be separated from God no matter what.

Take a look again at the diagram of a Saint with two souls (p.59). The same Adam mind, emotions, will & heart are still in a Saint…residue from the time of the Exchanged Life. Every Saint can wrestle with the same issues the Apostle Paul dealt with 2,000 years ago:

> For I know that in me, that is, in my flesh, dwelleth no good thing: for to will is present with me; but how to perform that which is good I find not. For the good that I would I do not: but the evil which I would not, that I do.
> Romans 7:18-19

A perfect example of living in the carnal soul, and a perfect lead to the victory in Christ/Holy Spirit (how to experiece that which is God). When the Saint abandons the carnal soul and abounds in the Holy Soul.

Every Saint is equipped to Live a perfect, sinless Life. Albeit it is God Living the perfect, sinless Life when He is given full and free reign.

d. Jesus Christ & a Saint

One of the missing elements of Scriptural teaching is the correct description of the Spiritual makeup of the Lord Jesus Christ in His *being* on earth. Perhaps the main reason is very few know and acknowledge that Jesus was *God in the flesh* (in an earthsuit). Many speak of this as Jesus being *made into being a man (or, human, as many erroneously say) in any proportion* by incorrect teaching, Truth has flown out the window. Haven't you heard things like *Jesus was 100% God & 100% man?* Or, *Jesus in His humanity…?* This immediately detours hearers from knowing and focusing on the Truthful Jesus. It deceives…it disguises…and it distorts Who Jesus in His earthsuit Truthfully was. He was God. No one else. Nothing else.

To teach that Jesus was a man in any proportion leads to Saints thinking in a humanistic way. *What would Jesus do?* This thinking leads to Saints trying to *be like Jesus.* Christianity is not us being like Jesus, but Jesus being Himself in our earthsuit. Try it. Live it. He Lives and He works.

Truth gives us the insight into the trichotomy of Jesus in an earthsuit. Holy Spirit was His Spirit. Holy Soul was His only Soul. And His Spirituality was housed inside His earthsuit.

A Saint is exactly the same likeness except for the additional soul. Saints now do not need to be told of our fellowship with God. We know it. And we know we can leave that fellowship very easily. Having 2 souls really opens that realization to great awareness.

Every Saint needs to get it sealed (by Holy Spirit) that we can never lose our *relationship* with God, but can lose our *fellowship*. Two very different matters. This leads to a relaxing *rest* of Life as a Saint.

Take a look again at the diagram of Jesus in an earthsuit on page 55. Other than an earthsuit (temporary house for Holy Spirit and Holy Soul…33 years) do you find ANY part that is *man?* No. Zero. And the suit does not make the man.

So let us be reminded there are two reasons for a Saint possessing *two souls* once we have been Born Again. There may be others, but these identify enough for us to be clear of the existence and the explanation of there being two souls in a Saint.

Think back to what is crucified at salvation, and what is created at salvation (take another close look at the trichotomy of a sinner, of a Saint, and of Jesus on earth). IF a Saint possesses ONLY the Holy Soul of his New Birth/New Creation, the Saint would have a trichotomy exactly like our Lord Jesus Christ had when He walked this earth in His earthsuit. This cannot be.

God also made a Saint dependent upon Him for Life the remaining days on this earth as a Saint. To *deny self* and *be dependent upon God* IS *Life as a Saint*. This all goes back to Who a Saint Truthfully is Spiritually after the New Birth/New Creation.

With our diagrams and an understanding of the *image* and *likeness* God speaks of in Genesis chapter 1 (and how that changes with the different manifestations since Creation), we can really start to delve into the two souls: their concept, their connection, their competition, and their conclusion (in eternity).

chapter 18

The HOLY Soul

For God who commanded the light to shine
out of darkness, hath shined in our hearts,
to give the light of the knowledge
of the glory of God in the face of Christ.
But we have this treasure in earthen vessels,
that the excellency of the power
may be of God, and not of us.
2 Corinthians 4:6-7

How many ever stop to mull on these 5 words, *the excellency of the power?* We know Who is the *power.* Holy Spirit. But think of that word *excellency.* It is from the Greek *huperbole.* Abundance, excellence, more exceedingly in the highest possible degree.

Where does Holy Spirit, the Power of God, manifest Himself? In His Holy Soul. *the excellency of the power* is seen, known, and experienced through Holy Soul. Holy Sound Mind. The set of Holy Emotions. Holy Will (Chooser). All equaling His Holy Heart.

The Holy Soul, albeit a mystery still to so many Saints, is everything to the functioning of the Life of a Saint. Its source is the Tree of Life. God. Always remember the Life of a Saint is Holy Spirit. His Life performed is through His Holy Soul. Therefore, why wouldn't we want to know of Holy Soul, know all there is to Holy Soul, and what Holy Soul means to each Saint? I know I do.

The Holy Soul houses the Holy Sound Mind of God, the set of Holy Emotions of God, and the Holy Will (Chooser) of God.

Think for a moment about the Holy Sound Mind of God. Omniscient. Knows all. There is not one single thing God's Holy Sound Mind does not know. That is almost more than we can imagine (if not thinking in the Mind of God in us). There is no limit to the extreme of Righteousness that the Holy Mind of God can think.

How do we figure what all God knows? He knows the names of every Saint. He knows the number of hairs on our head. He knows the names He has given to every star in the universe. And on and on…

God's set of His Holy Emotions in a Saint can be known in one word. LOVE. 1st Corinthians ch.13 tells us virtually all we need to know about Love and God's Holy Emotions. God is Love.

God's Will is not a plan, but that which He chooses and acts upon. The action and not the thought. He acts upon His plans, which are coming from His Holy Sound Mind. Sometimes His Will can be negated or detoured. The Holy Scriptures speak of *quenching* or *grieving* Holy Spirit.

For instance, the activity of God's Will can be quenched as when a sinner decides not to believe God and receive God's Eternal Life. God has told us He desires that ALL should be Saints:

> The Lord is not slack concerning his promise, as some men count slackness; but is long-suffering to us-ward, not willing that any should perish, but that all should come to repentance. 2 Peter 3:9

Scripture confirms God's plan including His deciding that any sinner who believes the record God has given of Jesus, trusts in Jesus' payment for their sin, and receives God's gift of Eternal Life, will be a child of God. But (an unholy but), if a sinner denies any one of the steps, the sinner remains separated from God and condemned to an eternity in Hell. The sinner has not made God's decision void, but has quenched what Holy Spirit could do.

Sadly, there are decisions made by us Saints that quench the work of Holy Spirit. Like when we know what the Word of God says, but we decide to do differently. Many, many times a Saint will read and know what God has said, but someone or something will take the Saint over to the unholy soul and the Will of God is not fulfilled. But (a Holy but) this cannot happen in the Holy Soul. Deciding against the Heart of God cannot happen in the Holy Soul. This confirms the importance of a Saint being diligent to stay in the Holy Soul as opposed to operating out of the unholy soul.

Any way in which we quench the work of Holy Spirit it grieves God. If we stop for just one moment and think about what God must be thinking every time one of us Saints decides to move from Holy Soul over into our unholy, carnal soul we would sense His grief. God's sadness and sorrow for one of His Saints to abandon trusting Him totally is a major thing. One of the prime factors in our fellowship with God is our total trust in Him. His Word. His Source of Life. His Power that He can show through our earthsuits. Think of all the ways in which we could grieve Him.

These two, quenching and grieving, keep us from enjoying the fullness of God in fellowship with Him.

I will never forget our pastor, John D. Morgan, preaching on Psalm 78 one Sunday shortly after we were Born Again. When he read v. 41, *yea, they turned back and tempted God, and limited the Holy One of Israel,* the summation of all their grieving thoughts and actions toward God...I wrote in the margin of my Bible: Putting the Handcuffs on God. God has led me to record many ways in which Saints today grieve God, limiting His power and actions in our lives. See my book titled *Putting the Handcuffs On God.*

Let us look again at the diagram showing the Holy Soul in a Saint (p. 59). And think about the particulars and the overall sum of the working of those particulars. God's Mind. Thoughts of the Omniscient One. Ours for the receiving. The thought and the power to take captive all the thoughts that are from the carnal mind. God's Emotions. Emotional control and perfect expression of Him enacting in every situation with every person. God's Will (Chooser). Taking the thoughts from Holy Mind and feelings from Holy Emotions and making Holy Choices yields the Holy Heart of God. Doesn't every Saint want the Heart of God to be what pours out of our earthsuits?

The thought that the Heart is the sum of the working of the Mind, Emotions, and Will/Chooser may be new to some. But take the time to look in a concordance and find that description perfectly fits where Heart is mentioned. For practical purposes the Heart identifies that which explains everything God does (His Grace). God's Grace is always aligned with God's Heart. They cannot be separated.

God's Heart gives us the sum of all the workings of the parts of the Holy Soul. Mind + Emotions + Will.

the unholy soul

And that ye may put difference
between holy and unholy,
and between clean and unclean.
Leviticus 10:10

But beloved, remember ye the words which were spoken
before of the apostles of our Lord Jesus Christ;
How that they told you there would be
mockers in the last time, who should
walk after their own ungodly lusts.
Jude 17-18

The antithesis of Holy Soul is the unholy soul. In a Saint, that remnant residue soul from a Saint's days as a sinner. The Truth that a Saint possesses that which is directly opposite of the perfection of God, although a Saint, is something many Saints never know or understand. They may be grieved themselves at what comes out of the unholy soul but not know of and fully understand how or why it is there.

Unholy soul. Sounds bad just saying those two words. The hell it creates in a Saint's Life is much more than bad. Its source is the fruit of the tree of the knowledge of good and evil, the tree God forbade Adam & Eve to eat from. And since it is connected to the devil, we must realize there is no limit to the extreme of evil the unholy mind in the unholy soul can think. There is no limit to the evil emotions or evil actions this soul can express through someone. And we must realize all of this is possible through the earthsuit of a Saint.

The unholy soul contains the natural mind, natural emotions, and natural will/decider…all under the influence of the devil. All enmity against God. Hell personified. Take a moment and look at the diagram of the unholy soul on p. 58.

Every evil thought, every evil word, every evil emotion, every evil decision comes from the unholy soul. What is horrific is the lack of teaching (if any) of a Saint possessing this residue spiritual soul. Just the lack of, or non-existent, teaching of this Truth is the work of the devil.

Have you ever noticed and been cognizant of the *fruit* of the tree of the knowledge of good and evil is parabolically what God is trying to teach us. Take a bite of the root. Sick! Take a bite of the trunk. Same thing. Take a bite of a branch. More of the same. But, take a bite of the fruit. Oh, that deceiving and distorting devil.

What thoughts go through our Holy Mind when we realize all the *good* thoughts and expressions are unholy? What thoughts go through our Holy Mind when we realize all the unholy emotions that spew forth from our earthsuit have their source in unholy soul? What thoughts go through our Holy Mind when we realize all the unholy choices and ultimate actions stem from the working of our unholy mind and unholy emotions we have been embracing? What thoughts go through our Holy Mind when we realize an unholy heart is inside our earthsuit?

Hang onto your seat! Remember what we have said all along exactly what *fruit* is? The ultimate expression of life. The *fruit* of the tree of knowledge of good and evil is the last remnant of expression of the devil in all Saints. A remnant that has some kick to it, even though the spiritual life of the devil has been removed at salvation. It is like watching something struggling and kicking and twisting as life passes. But we all know that kick still has some power to it. It is the *fruit* of the tree of the knowledge of good and evil that is so devastating. Not just the *knowledge* of the *fruit*. Eat and find destruction in one way or another.

We must never forget the devil's greatest ploy since the Garden of Eden... "Yea, hath God said...?" Look at the words from his encounter with Eve:

> Now the serpent was more subtle than any beast of the field which the LORD God had made. And he said unto the woman, Yea, hath God said, Ye shall not eat of every tree of the garden? And the woman said unto the serpent, We may eat of the fruit of the trees of the garden: But of the fruit of the tree which is in the midst of the garden, God hath said, Ye shall not eat of it, neither shall ye touch it, lest ye die. And the serpent said unto the woman, ye shall not surely die: For God doth know that in the day ye eat thereof, then your eyes shall be opened, and ye shall be

as gods, knowing good and evil. And when the woman saw that the tree was good for food, and that it was pleasant to the eyes, and a tree to be desired to make one wise, she took of the fruit thereof, and did eat, and gave also unto her husband with her; and he did eat. And the eyes of them both were opened, and they knew they were naked; and they sewed fig leaves together, and made themselves aprons. Genesis 3:1-7

It seems like every time I read these verses God shows me a new point. Even just now, two more new things right there in these verses that I don't believe I have ever noticed (or read/heard anyone identify). An entire book could be written on this passage.

What I must say here is that these seven verses are the epitome of the destruction the sinful, demonic, unholy soul can bring. Deceit, distortion, and detour from Truth are just an inkling of the devil's wiles. And we must notice the knowledge of the devil of some things never mentioned in Scripture prior to this moment.

I have a list of words that start with the letter "d." All that speak of the dastard actions the devil perpetrates upon the world, and in particular God's people.

I suppose I could mention the couple of things I see in this passage. One is that this is some of the most distinctly parabolic wording in the Holy Scriptures. Yes there are some things in the early chapters of Genesis that are beyond the natural mind (some of which are very important), but these words show the power of the god of this world (the devil), the destruction of innocence, and the disaster of the unholy soul. In addition, there are three things mentioned that are a parabolic picture of the great Truth presented in 1 John 2:16:

- the woman saw the tree was good for food (the lust of the flesh)
- and that it was pleasant to the eyes (and the lust of the eyes)
- and a tree to be desired to make one wise (and the pride of life)

It is remarkable how the Scripture is the best commentary on Scripture! Well, much time could be spent on the unholy soul. But that is not what I would draw our focus to. The Holy Soul is what we need to always seek, be drawn to, and stay focused on.

However, without the teaching of the *fruit* of this unholy soul for what it is, and what it does (and is capable of doing), a Saint not thinking and knowing he possesses the Holy Soul too often is left thinking of having some sort of generic, neutral spiritual soul. The next chapter will put to rest that lie from the pit of hell.

there is no neutral spiritual soul

He that is not with me is against me;
and he that scattereth not with me
scattereth abroad.
Matthew 12:30

No servant can serve two masters: for either
he will hate the one, and love the other;
or else he will hold to the one,
and despise the other.
Ye cannot serve God and mammon.
Luke 16:13

It is interesting there is no neutral spiritual soul. For one, there is no place for it to reside. All individuals are either a sinner or a Saint. There are no other options. There is no reason for a neutral spiritual soul to reside in either a sinner or a Saint. God has not planned for earth beings (who eventually become eternal beings in life after earth) to have a 3rd soul. There is no neutral eternal place. Heaven (Holy Soul) and hell (unholy soul).

There is no diagram of a trichotomy of a neutral person with a neutral soul. We cannot find any such thought in the Holy Scriptures.

Therefore, we must not try to explain away any actions that are of the unholy soul. Unholy is unholy, and demonic. We really should not try to take any praise for the actions of the Holy Soul. Any Holiness or Righteousness that springs from the Holy Soul in a Saint is God's work, God's doing.

Let me run an idea by you…there is no *man* since the early days of the Creation of Adam & Eve. They were innocent beings. The only *man* on earth. Not righteous. Not sinful. Simply *innocent man*. With their sin, *innocent man* became *sinful man,* a sinner according to God. There has been no *innocent man* ever since. With salvation, a *sinner man* became Born Again (Spiritually Born through Holy Spirit) into a *righteous man,* a Saint…Holy. What other *man* is there? None. No one is just *man*.

Knowing this, we should not talk about *man* doing anything, *man* thinking anything, *man* this, and *man* that. Can you see how this negates Truth about two souls? Can you see how so many Saints look upon themselves still as a sinner? No. God never speaks of His Saints as being sinners. Only Holy. Only Righteous. That is why 61 times in the N.T. Holy Spirit Himself chose *Saint* in identifying a child of God. And only 3 times does the word *Christian* appear! Not once where God spoke of His children as being Christian(s).df

All throughout the Holy Scriptures we see the word *man*. But how often have we taken the time and effort to look up the Hebrew and Greek words that are translated *man?* They always are identifying a generic earth being, or male, or a group of such beings. And most likely a mistake of the translators choosing to not use the two terms of each *man*. Two terms which identify *which man*. Try using the two terms in verses where *man* appears. It can be eye-opening to really Seeing what God is saying.

Once Saints know and refuse to think there is some sort of generic neutral soul, or generic neutral being, Truth begins to spring forth showing the actions and interaction of Saints and sinners. A new understanding of all things of life come into focus. A new appreciation springs forth for God gifting a repenting sinner trusting Jesus Christ as Savior (nothing or no one else) with Holy Spirit and Holy Soul. What a plan. His Will realized. It is done.

We have come near the end of the book…almost. Four short chapters left. All having to do with identifying Life, the Life of God, expressed in terms not usually seen. In fact in many Christian circles these terms are avoided, if not forbidden. And yet, they provide the clear picture of exactly what Life as a Saint is, in a unique way.

chapter 21

Double-souled, Double-minded

A double-minded man is unstable
in all his ways.
James 1:8

This verse on the surface makes immediate sense. Anyone who is past the early teen years knows that *a flip-flopping mind* causes lots of issues. Being *unstable* is one of them most are familiar with.

How many people, Saints included, seem to spend all their time *flip-flopping* back and forth on an issue…often never able to make up their mind! The question is: which mind? And here is something so many are not aware of: the *carnal mind* in Saints has *two sides*. From the *tree of the knowledge of good and evil*, it can one minute be thinking *good* things, and then the next minute flip and be thinking *evil* things, or some variance of either that causes a lot of the *flip-flopping* from those thinking in the *carnal mind*.

Some of you may be thinking, *I just have a problem trying to decide in my physical brain on an issue that is not spiritual.* What we must know is that *the spiritual mind can impact what the physical brain thinks.* That adds importance to Saints thinking in the *Mind of God* and not in the *carnal mind*.

But here is another issue: this is another one of the *parabolic* verses personified, and God's Truth gives explanation and clarification to all we have said so far. One of the beauties of the trichotomy diagram of a Saint (p. 59) is the clear picture of the *battle lines* in Saints. Know this. There is never a battle in a Saint's Spirit. Flip-flopping between the two minds.

The English word *double-minded* leads most to simply think of how a person can *change their mind* from one minute to the next on an issue. The Greek is one word, *dipsuchos*. It literally means *twice souled/twice minded*. What? Two souls/two minds? Yes. Right there in the original language. Two souls. Two minds. Whoa! That takes us back to the importance of the Scriptural diagram of the trichotomy of a Saint.

Until we see ourselves for who we really are, there is no way to deal with the *double-mindedness* so many experience. Any battle comes from war between the two souls. Victory always comes from single-Mindedness in the Holy Soul.

chapter 22

Be Not Self-deceived

But be ye doers of the word,
and not hearers only,
deceiving your own selves.
James 1:22

We not only deal with being *double-souled, double-minded...flip-flopping* from one mind to the other, we now deal with another thought: *deceiving ourselves.* How? *Deception can only come from the carnal mind.* Period. Never in the *Mind of God.* Once again, understanding the diagram of a Saint's trichotomy sealed in our thoughts leads to victory and the Way to end *self-deception.* Look at some more in James that Holy Spirit gives on this...

> For if any be a hearer of the word, and not a doer, he is like unto a man beholding his natural face in a glass: For he beholdeth himself, and goeth his way, and straightway forgetteth what manner of man he was. But whoso looketh into the perfect law of liberty, and continueth therein, he being not a forgetful hearer, but a doer of the work, this man shall be blessed in his deed. 1:23-25

One more passage before the final thoughts...

> Yea, a man may say, Thou hast faith, and I have works: show me thy faith without thy works, and I will show thee my faith by my works. Thou believest that there is one God; thou doest well: the devils also believe, and tremble. But wilt thou know, O vain man, that faith without works is dead? 2:18-20

God never says that someone is not a Saint IF they do not have *works.* That would go against the foundational fundamental Truth that being a Saint is a *birth,* not a *work of ourselves.*

However, does any Saint believe the Life of God could be in our earthsuit and (1) not want to do His works, and/or (2) not see that His Faith/Life does His works?

That is why He tells us to not be deceived *by being hearers only of His Word.* That's a parabolic saying in itself...catch it?

chapter 23

The 3 Lives of Saints

I am crucified with Christ: nevertheless I live;
yet not I, but Christ liveth in me:
and the life which I now live in the flesh
I live by the faith of the Son of God,
who loved me, and gave himself for me
Galatians 2:20

The three Lives experienced while still on earth. Three great parabolic teachings. In these we see the answer to three most important questions all must answer (all wrapped up in our text verse):

1. What of the old man is crucified at the moment of salvation?
2. What is created in the new Saint at that same moment?
3. How is the New Creation experienced?

the EXCHANGED LIFE

For ye are dead, and your life is hid with Christ in God. When Christ, who is our life, shall appear, then shall ye also appear with him in glory. Colossians 3:3-4

He answered and said, Whether he be a sinner or no, I know not: one thing I know, that, whereas I was blind, now I see. John 9:25

Therefore if any man be in Christ, he is a new creature: old things are passed away; behold, all things are become new. 2 Corinthians 5:17

A very unique and perfectly descriptive word of the exact moment of salvation. *Exchanged* does not appear in Scripture, but becoming a *new creation* gives Heavenly meaning to the Heavenly Truth of the *old, sinful life of a sinner* being exchanged by the *Holy Life of God in a Saint*.

There are a multitude of ways this exchange could be expressed. All Scriptural. One of the neatest challenges is to be alert as we read Scripture and note when the Exchanged Life is mentioned (almost always parabolically in other terms). Can you see the possibilities by the verses given?

So much of the post-Pentecost writings of the New Testament speak of the old life and then the new Life. That is an exchange. And they speak as Paul did in Colossians of *we Live, but it is not us.* Holy Spirit spoke parabolically saying *For ye are dead, and your life is hid with Christ in God.* That kind of writing twists the natural and carnal minds to try and explain. It is simple. A sinner's life has been crucified. Dead. But the Saint has a Life. It is the Life of God. That was easy, wasn't it?

John 9 speaks of the time when Jesus anointed the eyes of one born blind. This could have been the beginning of the Spittites. Jesus spat on the ground, made some clay of where he had spat, and stuck that onto the eyes of the blind one. Then of all the ways God has exchanged the old life with the new Life this one takes the cake, as my grandma Bradford used to say. Jesus sent the fellow away to the pool of Siloam, and said *Wash in the pool.* The guy did. Stood up. Saw. *Came seeing* Scripture says. Many saw that he saw. His parents were astounded. They said *He is of age, ask him.* Ultimately the Pharisees couldn't stand it. They brought him forth and said to him, *Give God the praise; we know that this man is a sinner (v. 24).* It was testimony time! And Holy Spirit gives his testimony in verse 25. It was all Jesus.

My wife, Barbara, and I were Born Again in Pastor John Morgan's office at Sagemont Church in Houston on Tuesday, May 20, 1980. The very first words out of Pastor Morgan's mouth after we each had prayed to trust the Lord Jesus Christ as our very own personal Savior were to show us in Scripture what just took place. He read 2 Corinthians 5:17. A new creature. The old life had passed away. The new Life had come into being by the Supernatural Spiritual work of Holy Spirit.

Many folks think this verse tells us that all our old sins have to stop, pass away. Not Truth. The unholy, carnal soul has made sure of that. The parabolic Truth is that *all Spiritual things are new, beginning with the new Life (Holy Spirit) and new expressions (Holy Soul).* Lovely parabolic Truth. There is no Life like the Life of God. There is nothing to compare with possessing the Life of God in an earthsuit.

Thank God for the EXCHANGED LIFE. Glory! Hallelujah!

the ABIDING LIFE

> I AM the true vine, and my Father is the husbandman.
> …Abide in me, and I in you. As the branch cannot bear
> fruit of itself, except it abide in the vine; no more can ye,
> except ye abide in me. I am the vine, ye are the branches:
> He that abideth in me, and I in him, the same bringeth
> forth much fruit: for without me ye can do nothing.
> John 15:1, 4-5

Let us not miss the *fruit* of this Vine, the Lord Jesus Christ. His Life. Abiding is to be a branch (available 24/7/52) for the Life of God to flow through us to produce His *Fruit*, His Life for us to know and experience. Also for others to see it.

The Greek *meno* is translated *abide/abiding* in the English. It means to *remain, dwell*. In John's writings it means one person remains with another. This one word describes the eternality of a Saint being Born Again and always, forever, being in the Family of God. Beautiful. *Once saved, always saved* many Saints like to say. Truth.

Meno is also translated *continueth, dwelleth, endureth*. All meaning to *remain*. It is also applied to the Life of God remaining in a Saint, as in *The Word*. Or, God's *Fruit*.

It is a sad day to encounter a Saint struggling with whether they truthfully are a Saint. Too much bad life, too much false preaching, too much false teaching, too much reading of the Holy Scriptures in the carnal mind can lead a Saint to doubt their salvation. The good news is what Dr. Hal Boone, Minister of Missions, once told me at Sagemont Church back in 1984: *Only a Saint will ever doubt their salvation. It takes being one to doubt whether you are one.* I can testify that until Holy Spirit convicted me of being a sinner I never doubted whether or not I was a Saint. The devil had led me to one thought of deception: *No matter what your life is like, down deep you are a good guy. And surely God wouldn't send a good guy to hell.* Of course there were times I thought *I hope I am going to Heaven when I die.* Never doubted as in knowing Truth about The Way or whether I had been Born Again.

Being a branch and remaining have to do with the *Life of God* abiding in a Saint. And the Saint abiding in the *Life of God*.

Thank God for the ABIDING LIFE. Glory! Hallelujah!

> For I am the least of the apostles, that am not meet to be called an apostle, because I persecuted the church of God. But by the grace of God I am what I am: and his grace which was bestowed upon me was not in vain: but I labored more abundantly than they all: yet not I, but the grace of God which was with me. 1 Corinthians 15:9-10

In this spectacular announcement the Apostle Paul makes two definitive statements: (1) because of his actions prior to being a Saint he was dastard in his persecution of the church of God. This Saint we all love to know and appreciate was the lead guy watching over the murder of Stephen. He made havoc of the church, Scripture says.

And yet, we know of his marvelous conviction, conversion, and calling to be a Saint and ultimately the writer of 13 books of the New Testament. This is where Paul's second declaration comes in, (2) he gives God credit for any calling, any position, any Spiritual victory, everything Spiritual. And Holy Spirit gives us the incredible parabolic statement of I AM again.

But by the grace of God I am what I am. These I am's are not to be taken lightly or overlooked. It was I AM who did the work of salvation and calling and ministering through the earthsuit of Paul. Anything of any Saint Spiritually is from the Great I AM. We can join Paul in declaring *I am what I am by the grace (doing) of God.*

How many of us have tried, made all efforts, sweated and toiled, perhaps secretly, to make changes in our lives? All to no avail. And unless we turn it over to God and tell Him that if He doesn't do something, if He doesn't show up, we will continue to fail miserably. Ah, the Presence of God. There is nothing the Presence of God cannot do. Matthew 19:26 tells us this:

> But Jesus beheld them, and said unto them, With men this
> is impossible; but with God all things are possible.

That's Grace. That is the GRACE LIFE.

The Greek charis is translated *grace* in the English. It means that which *God does* when speaking in any way of the *Grace of God.* Many make *grace* a nebulous word by giving it a meaning of *God's unmerited favor.* In Christianity, what isn't an unmerited favor…especially anything God has given us?

The great wonder of Christianity is that each Saint can experience the *Life of God* through our physical earthsuit. We can experience freedom from any bondage our enemy may have over us. We can experience the power, provision, and protection of the Presence of God in us. God Living through a Saint's earthsuit is a marvel to behold.

There is nothing the GRACE LIFE can't provide.

Thank God for the GRACE LIFE. Glory! Hallelujah!

chapter 24

LIFE as a Saint
Experiencing the Heavenly Truth
of parabolic teaching

If ye then be risen with Christ,
seek those things which are above,
where Christ sitteth on the right hand of God.
Set your affections on things above,
not on things on the earth.
For ye are dead, and your life
is hid with Christ in God.
When Christ, who is our life, shall appear,
then shall ye also appear with him in glory.
Colossians 3:1-4

The Spiritual Life of a Saint has a beginning (creation), a continuation in this dispensation (abiding), and an enjoyment (God's Grace). We saw the reality of these in Chapter 23, The 3 Lives of Saints. There is more than just the fact of these 3 Lives…there is the experiencing of them.

Before we close out the book it is worth looking at some verses again that have been mentioned. A quick summary and analysis. And celebrate these powerful Truths once more.

BEGINNING

Everything in Christianity begins with Truth…God/Jesus/Holy Spirit.
Ye shall know the truth, and the truth shall make you free…If the Son therefore shall make you free, ye shall be free indeed. John 8:32, 36

Thomas saith unto him, Lord, we know not whither thou goest; and how can we know the way? Jesus saith unto him, I am the way, the truth, and the life: no man cometh unto the Father, but by me. John 14:5-6

Philip saith unto him, Lord, show us the Father, and it sufficeth us. Jesus saith unto him, Have I been so long time with you, and yet hast thou not known me, Philip? he that hath seen me hath seen the Father; and how sayest thou then, Show us the Father? Believest thou not that I am in the Father, and the Father in me? the words that I speak unto you I speak not of myself: but the Father that dwelleth in me, he doeth the works. John 14:8-10

And I will pray the Father, and he shall give you another Comforter, that he may abide with you for ever; Even the Spirit of truth; whom the world cannot receive, because it seeth him not, neither knoweth him: but ye know him; for he dwelleth with you, and shall be in you. John 14:16-17

And there is salvation…

As it is written, There is on righteous, no, not one: there is none that understandeth, there is none that seeketh after God…For all have sinned, and come short of the glory of God. Romans 3:10-11, 23

For when we were yet without strength, in due time Christ died for the ungodly. For scarcely for a righteous man will one die: yet peradventure for a good man some would even dare to die. But God commendeth his love toward us, in that, while we were yet sinners, Christ died for us. Romans 5:6-8

And the keeper of the prison…called for a light, and sprang in, and came trembling, and fell down before Paul and Silas, And brought them out, and said, Sirs, what must I do to be saved? And they said, Believe on the Lord Jesus Christ, and thou shalt be saved, and thy house. Acts 16:27, 29-31

But the righteousness which is of faith speaketh on this wise…That if thou wilt confess with thy mouth the Lord

Jesus, and shalt believe in thine heart that God hath raised him from the dead, thou shalt be saved. For with the heart man believeth unto righteousness; and with the mouth confession is made unto salvation…For whosoever shall call upon the name of the Lord shall be saved. Romans 10:6, 9-10, 13

CONTINUATION

There is LIFE after salvation, until God calls us Home for the rest of Eternity. The Life here on earth is Life as a Saint. However we must be clear, this Life is not of a Saint, but 100% of God. It is the Life of God Lived through a Saint's earthsuit. Life as a Saint of God.

And such were some of you: but ye are washed, but yea are sanctified, but ye are justified in the name of the Lord Jesus, and by the Spirit of our God. 1 Corinthians 6:11

For ye were sometimes darkness, but now are ye light in the Lord: walk as children of light: For the fruit of the Spirit is in all goodness and righteousness and truth; Proving what is acceptable unto the Lord. Ephesians 5:8-10

The thief cometh not, but for to steal, and to kill, and to destroy: I am come that they might have life, and that they might have it more abundantly. John 10:10

This I say then, Walk in the Spirit, and ye shall not fulfill the lust of the flesh…But if ye be led of the Spirit, ye are not under the law…But the fruit of the Spirit is love, joy, peace, long-suffering, gentleness, goodness, faith, Meekness, temperance: against such there is no law. And they that are Christ's have crucified the flesh with the affections and lusts. If we live in the Spirit, let us also walk in the Spirit. Galatians 5:16, 18, 22-25

For we are his workmanship, created in Christ Jesus unto good works, which God hath before ordained that we should walk in them. Ephesians 2:10

What about the difference between law, works, belief, and faith? Where do each of these fit into Life as a Saint?

And when they had found him on the other side of the sea, they said unto him, Rabbi, when camest thou hither? Jesus answered them and said, Verily, verily, I say unto you, ye seek me, not because ye saw the miracles, but because ye did eat of the loaves, and were filled. Labor not for the meat which perisheth, but for that meat which endureth unto everlasting life, which the Son of man shall give unto you: for him hath God the Father sealed. Then said they unto him, What shall we do, that we might work the works of God? Jesus answered and said unto them, This is the work of God, that ye believe on him whom he hath sent. John 6:25-29

We having the same spirit of faith, according as it is written, I believed, and therefore have I spoken; we also believe, and therefore speak. 2 Corinthians 4:13

For if our heart condemn us, God is greater than our heart, and knoweth all things...And this is his commandment, That we should believe on the name of his Son Jesus Christ, and love one another, as he gave us commandment. 1 John 2:20, 23

He that believeth on the Son of God hath the witness in himself: he that believeth not God hath made him a liar; because he believeth not the record that God gave of his Son. And this is the record, that God hath given to us eternal life, and this life is in his Son. He that hath the Son hath life; and he that hath not the Son of God hath not life. These things have I written unto you that believe on the name of the Son of God; that ye may know that ye

have eternal life, and that ye may believe on the name of
the Son of God. 1 John 5:10-13

Believing is the work of every earth being. Faith cannot be obtained by
work.

We hear a lot of people saying, "You just need to have faith." Or, "You
need to have more faith." If we turn that around to ourselves, it will sound
like, "I need to have faith in this matter." "I need to have more faith."
What does God say about this?

But the fruit of the Spirit is…faith… Galatians 5:22
This one verse puts an end to earth beings, sinners or Saints, doing any
work to obtain faith. Scriptural Faith is beyond earth. It is Spiritual. Of
God. There is much more…

Now faith is the substance of things hoped for, the
evidence of things not seen. Hebrews 11:1

But without faith it is impossible to please him: for he that
cometh to God must believe that he is, and that he is a
rewarder of them that diligently seek him. Hebrews 11:6

But now the righteousness of God without the law is
manifested, being witnessed by the law and the prophets
Even the righteousness of God which is by faith of Jesus
Christ unto all and upon all them that believe: for there is
no difference. Romans 3:21-22

Knowing that a man is not justified by the works of the
law, but by the faith of Jesus Christ, even we have believed
in Jesus Christ, that we might be justified by the faith of
Christ, and not by the works of the law: for by the works
of the law shall no flesh be justified. Galatians 2:16

But what things were gain to me, those I counted loss for
Christ. Yea doubtless, and I count all things but loss for
the excellency of the knowledge of Christ Jesus my Lord:
for whom I have suffered the loss of all things, and do

count them but dung, that I may win Christ, and be found in him, not having mine own righteousness, which is of the law, but that which is through the faith of Christ, the righteousness which is of God by faith. Philippians 3:7-9

Buried with him in baptism, wherein ye are risen with him through the faith of the operation of God, who hath raised him from the dead. Colossians 2:12

Looking unto Jesus the author and finisher of our faith; who by the joy that was set before him endured the cross, despising the shame, and is set down at the right hand of the throne of God. Hebrews 12:2

ENJOYMENT

We have talked about the Grace Life, God's Grace being experienced and enjoyed all our days on earth. Nothing says it more explicitly than Holy Spirit's explanation of His Living through the Apostle Paul. Paul speaking of what was done through his earthsuit, but it wasn't Paul doing it.

For I am the least of the apostles, that am not meet to be called an apostle, because I persecuted the church of God. But by the grace of God I am what I am: and his grace which was bestowed upon me was not in vain: but I labored more abundantly than they all: yet not I, but the grace of God which was with me. 1 Corinthians 15:9-10

This is the enjoyment God wants us to experience. Not complicated, Not really complex. Simple. Believe, trust, and receive.

With the Life of God and His Grace we can experience and enjoy all His Life has to offer.

Put on therefore, as the elect of God, holy and beloved, bowels of mercies, kindness, humbleness of mind, meekness, long-suffering; Forbearing one another, and forgiving one another, if any man have a quarrel against any: even as Christ forgave you, so also do ye. Colossians 3:12-13

Notice the *put on's* are all Fruit of Holy Spirit. God does the *putting on* if it is done. All *works* by God through our earthsuit? God doing the doing. Just as He did in Jesus' earthsuit. His Grace.

> Believest thou not that I am in the Father, and the Father in me? the words that I speak unto you I speak not of myself: but the Father that dwelleth in me, he doeth the works. John 14:10

One other thing we must see done while travelling this terra firma. Forgive all. Barbara and I came up with a great saying back in the pastoring days. *I cannot not forgive.*

God is the greatest forgiver of all. In fact, He has said that only *blaspheming against the Holy Spirit* is the only unforgiveable sin.

> Wherefore I say unto you, All manner of sin and blasphemy shall be forgiven unto men: but the blasphemy against the Holy Ghost, shall not be forgiven unto men. And whosoever speaketh a word against the Son of man, it shall be forgiven him: but whosoever speaketh against the Holy Ghost, it shall not be forgiven him, neither in this world, neither in the world to come. Matthew 12:31-32

As far as our forgiving someone for anything and everything, God is adamant about our *always* forgiving.

> And when ye stand praying, forgive, if ye have aught against any: that your Father also which is in heaven may forgive you your trespasses. Mark 11:25

> For if we forgive men their trespasses, your heavenly Father will also forgive you. But if ye forgive not men their trespasses, neither will your Father forgive your trespasses. Matthew 6:14-15

Remember…

> Put on therefore, as the elect of God, holy and beloved, bowels of mercies, kindness, humbleness of mind, meekness, long-suffering; Forbearing one another, and forgiving one another, if any man have a quarrel against any: even as Christ forgave you, so also do ye. Colossians 3:12-13

Therefore, is there ANY trespass or reason we are not to forgive? None. Albeit it is God doing the forgiving through our earthsuit. We must adopt the saying and experience God's Grace to say, *I cannot not forgive*. Unforgiveness is unacceptable to God.

So…while God is doing all the doing/working, what does He tell us to do? REST.

> Come unto me, all ye that labor and are heavy laden, and
> I will give you rest. Take my yoke upon you, and learn of
> me; for I am meek and lowly in heart: and ye shall find rest
> unto your souls. For my yoke is easy, and my burden is
> light. Matthew 11:28-30

REST. Enjoy Life as a Saint. Enjoy all the Supernatural Spiritual *work* God does through us.

Chapter 25

From Here to Eternity

Behold, I show you a mystery;
we shall not all sleep,
but we shall all be changed.
1 Corinthians 15:51

This final chapter will look at From Here to Eternity. A brief look at some verses that speak of Saints moving into Eternity with God.

> For God so loved the world, that he gave his only begotten Son, that whosoever believeth in him should not perish, but have everlasting life. John 3:16

> Verily, verily, I say unto you, He that heareth my word, and believeth on him that sent me, hath everlasting life, and shall not come into condemnation; but is passed from death unto life. John 5:24

> But whosoever drinketh of the water that I shall give him shall never thirst; but the water that I shall give him shall be in him a well of water springing up into everlasting life. John 4:14

> And this is the promise that he hath promised us, even eternal life. 1 John 2:25

> But grow in grace, and in the knowledge of our Lord and Savior Jesus Christ. To him be glory both now and for ever. Amen. 2 Peter 3:18

Eternity is a long time. Finite mind cannot comprehend how long that is. But it is a long time. Everyone either spends that long time with the devil in hell, or with God in Heaven.

1 Corinthians 15 is a great chapter to study. It starts in verses 1-4 with the Gospel of the Lord Jesus Christ. It continues with great thoughts about the Grace of God, including Paul's fabulous discourse in verses 8-11. Then Holy Spirit moves to talking about the crucifixion and Christ rising from the dead. But in the last 39 verses God gives us a magnificent look at moving from earth here and now to Eternity.

The *after*-Life. Life with God in Heaven. The Life of days that cannot be numbered. Very little preaching, teaching, and writing speak of this Eternal Life. There may be lots of mentioning it, but not much expounding and detailing just how Saints will be when we reach Heaven.

I started *The Images of God & Man,* the book that is the predecessor to this one, by asking one question of God: How am I going to actually GET to Heaven? That led to another: What am I going to BE LIKE in Heaven?

I knew I was going to Heaven. I knew there would be a wonderful Eternal Life in Heaven. I knew that only Saints will be with God in Heaven. But I did not know how I was *actually* going to get there, and what I would actually be like when I got there. God always has answers to questions we ask of Him.

I knew a couple of verses that gave some indication of our Heavenly makeup.

> For now we see through a glass, darkly; but then face to face: now I know in part; but then shall I know even as also I am known. 1 Corinthians 13:12

> Beloved, now are we the sons of God, and it doth not yet appear what we shall be: but we know that, when he shall appear, we shall be like him: for we shall see him as he is. 1 John 3:2

Who would have dreamed we would end up in Heaven being *like God? As He is.* That's what God says. Do we believe Him?

Let's look at a couple of other verses that give more of the picture.

> So also is the resurrection of the dead. It is sown in corruption; it is raised in incorruption: It is sown in dishonor; it is raised in glory: it is sown in weakness; it is raised in power: It is sown a natural body; it is raised a spiritual body. There is a natural body, and there is a spiritual body. 1 Corinthians 15:42-44

Then there are the words that come right after our text verse for the chapter.

> In a moment, in the twinkling of an eye, at the last trump: for the trumpet shall sound, and the dead shall be raised incorruptible, and we shall be changed. For this corruptible must put on incorruption, and this mortal must put on immortality. So when this corruptible shall have put on incorruption, and this mortal shall have put on immortality, then shall be brought to pass the saying that is written, Death is swallowed up in victory...thanks be to God, which giveth us the victory through our Lord Jesus Christ. I Corinthians 15:52-54, 57

Take another look at the diagram on p. 61, the diagram of Saints in Heaven. Beginning with 1 soul (an unholy soul), to having 2 souls (unholy and Holy), back to 1 soul (Holy Soul). What a parabolic adventure.

From here on earth to Eternity with God. Just as He is. BUT...not God. Simply His Image and Likeness as never before. A parable for sure.

appendix

Examples of Misleading Theology
the culprit: the natural, carnal mind

This is a summary of things that have been covered
in this book, but need to be emphasized once more,
and to strongly encourage Truthful use
of words that belong to God.

Saints and sinners alike often express erroneous and misleading Scriptural theology because of the disguises, deceptions, diversions, and distortions coming out of the natural (sinner) and carnal (Saint) minds. God has clearly revealed the blindness and prohibition of Truth being known to these two minds (same mind, different beings).

May God bring about a revival of His thoughts, His words, His diagrams, His Truth by a Holy Spirit revelation to all Saints who can see, hear, and know Truth. The following information is to once again draw attention to some key ways the arch enemy of God, the devil, whom God has declared to be *the god of this world,* uses his greatest tool: *Yea, hath God said?*

Much benefit will come from soaking on the Truth present here…

wrong definitions lead to wrong statements and explanations
- creation
- created in image of God
- faith & believe
- Grace of God

Millions have been detoured from the crucial realization that only God can *create.* Man can *make,* but not create. To create is to bring something into being that has never before existed. All of creation mentioned in the first chapters of Genesis. To carelessly let Divine words take on humanistic meaning distorts Truth.

Only Adam & Eve were *created* in the image & likeness of God. All others since have been *begat.* To stop for a moment and realize the absolute

Truth of this gives more power and life to *creation*. God *created* Adam & Eve. God designed all others like Adam & Eve to be *made, begat, conceived* by male & female…starting with Cain & Abel. This realization removes all the talk about *ALL of us have been created in the image of God*. Many include sinners as such.

It is very interesting and important to know and realize that God *creates* again when a new Saint is Born. Scripture points out different ways a Saint is a *creation*. Again, using this term correctly identifies the work of God, and He gets proper recognition and credit.

Faith and *believe* are not the same thing. Two different words, from two different sources, with two totally different meanings and usages. However, millions use *Faith* and *believe* as if they are the same thing. Doing so eliminates the Divine of Faith (Fruit of Holy Spirit/ultimate expression of God's Life), and reduces the term to a humanistic action. *Believe* is the work sinners and Saints are to do. God cannot *believe*. He IS Truth and Omniscience.

The *Grace of God* is a term meaning the work of God, His doing. Yes, it is an undeserved and unmerited favor, but it is Who is doing the doing that needs to be known and emphasized. Which leads to Saints knowing all the Spiritual is God's doing. We bring nothing to the table, except what He has done. I am what I am by the *Grace of God* (His working/His doing). And so are you.

wrong diagrams of man
- dichotomy of sinners & Saints
- faulty trichotomy illustrations

For the last 40 years I have been searching and researching *diagrams* made trying to show the makeup of sinners and Saints. The findings have been exasperating. Only one *diagram* has made any sense, except it has been used to show sinners and Saints as being exactly the same…which is a lie spiritually.

A careful and extensive review of chapter 11 is critical to getting the makeup of all beings (God, sinners, and Saints) correct. These are very important *diagrams,* very important information. They give Truth from eternity past to eternity future.

And without knowing the Truthful *diagrams,* so much false teaching and preaching is showered upon unknowing Saints. And disguises, deceptions, and distortions abound…rendering Saints wandering in the wilderness not discovering the great Truthful connections between God and mankind, in all the dispensations God has ordained.

One great distortion worth mentioning and explaining is that of earth beings being a *dichotomy.* The idea that all mankind is a *dichotomy* (2 parts…spirit/soul & body) is false theology. Two questions destroy any idea of being a *dichotomy.* 1) at salvation, what of a sinner is crucified and removed? Answer: the *demonic, Adam spirit*…the change from the innocent spirit of Adam in the Garden to Adam after the Fall. That *spirit* is *crucified,* life ended, and removed from the individual being created a new Saint. 2) at salvation, what is the new *creation* God tells us of? He *creates* in the new Saint His *Holy Spirit and His Holy Soul.*

Nothing shows the Truth any better that God leaves the *unholy soul* (a separate entity/part of a sinner) IN the new Saint at salvation than Romans chapters 6, 7, & 8. The perfect illustration of Saints being a trichotomy. A careful reading and studying shows that *spirit* and *soul* cannot be one entity, as a dichotomist teaches.

It is sad experts and well-meaning theological scholars have long disparaged and destroyed their own declaration that mankind is a dichotomy. They have long stated that God is only a Spirit (a *monogamy-chotomy?),* never mentioning God has a soul, or heavensuit. And that mankind is a *dichotomy* (spirit/soul & body). Yet, mankind is *created* in the *image and likeness of God.* Do you see the deceived carnal mind at work?

wrong explanations of verses

The list of such verses is almost innumerable. With false definitions and false diagrams, and the lack of knowing, understanding, believing, and receiving the parabolic teaching of ALL Spiritual Truth in the Holy Scriptures, how much Truthful understanding exists among the Saints?

using nebulous singular words (not knowing 2 souls)

- soul
- mind
- heart

Albeit God has Divinely inspired the Holy Scriptures to be word for word perfect, Saints experiencing the lack of seeing, hearing, recognizing, and knowing the absolute difference of the two spiritual souls, two spiritual minds, and two spiritual hearts renders chaos and confusion to unlimited extremes. It is imperative to KNOW which soul, which mind, and which heart God is speaking of when these words appear in the Holy Scriptures.

If you will stop long enough to give it much thought, you will discover there are many uses of singular words in Scripture that do not identify one or more entities that exist of the one word. Stay alert in the Lord when reading or listening to the Holy Scriptures. God has some incredible Truth that can go unknown if not functioning in Holy Soul.

A parting word…

One Truth that all Saints can agree on: God is Truth. God is revealing Truth to His Saints in these Last Days. This all occurs in the Mind of God within the Saint.

As insanity in the natural and carnal minds expands and explodes upon mankind world-wide, Truth will be the cornerstone of Love, Joy, Peace, Long-suffering, Gentleness, Goodness, Faith, Meekness, and Temperance experienced and exposed through the Saints who are so abandoned and depending upon God, and whose Heart is God's Heart revealed on all matters and in all instances.

May we pray for an out-pouring of Holy Spirit upon ALL Saints to See, Know, and Experience God/Truth as we look to the coming of our Lord Jesus Christ.

Scripture References

verse	page #		verse	page #
Genesis			**Proverbs**	
1:1	47,85		2:10	28,48
1:11-12	63		11:14	70
1:26-27	42,49,86		12:15	70
1:27	50		19:20-21	69
1:29	63		**Isaiah**	
2:9	34,36,39,63		28:9-10	24
2:16-17	63,64		47:4	47
3:1	64		**Jeremiah**	
3:1-7	96		23:24	48
3:7-8	87		**Lamentations**	
3:22-24	40		3:20	28
5:1,3-5	76		**Daniel**	
5:1-3	49		2:29	48
5:3	50		**Hosea**	
Leviticus			4:6	70
10:10	94		11:9	48
Judges			**Matthew**	
10:16	28		1:23	47
1 Chronicles			6:14-15	113
22:19	28		11:25-27	11,15
Job			11:28-30	114
6:7	28		12:30	98
7:15	28		12:31-32	113
30:25	28		13:1-3	44
Psalm			13:1-9	37,78
42:1	28		13:3-9	18,19
55:22	47		13:10-17	19,47,78
86:4	28		13:10-23	37
147:5	48		13:11-12,16	79,83

Scripture References (cont'd)

verse	page #	verse	page #
Matthew		**John**	
13:24-30	19	6:44	45
13:34	17	6:54-56	64
13:34-35	37,46,47	8:32,36	107
19:26	105	ch. 9	103
23:9	47	9:25	102
24:14	85	10:10	109
28:18-20	22	10:37-38	12
Mark		10:38	15
4:1-9	37	14:5-6	107
4:10-34	37	14:6	127
10:18	35	14:6-7	45
11:25	113	14:10	108,113
13:31-32	85	14:16	47
Luke		14:16-17	108
2:25	15	14:27	28,82
2:25-26	12	15:1,4-5	104
6:47-48	24	15:5	48
10:24	15	15:11	28
10:21-24	12	17:26	47
12:2	12,15	**Acts**	
16:13	98	5:14	32
18:13	48	11:26	32
18:19	35	16:27,29-31	108
John		26:28	32
1:11-12	127	**Romans**	
3:3-7	127	1:7	48
3:16	115	1:16-18	12
4:14	115	3:10	87
5:24	115	3:10-11	76,108
6:25-29	110	3:21-22	111

Scripture References (cont'd)

verse	page #
Romans	
3:23	76,87,108
5:6-8	108
5:8	87
5:12-14,18,19	76
ch's 6-8	70,119
6:6	66,67
6:12	67
7:15-17	20
7:18-19	89
7:20-25	80
8:6-7	47,73,74,80
8:7	28
8:9	26,27,88
8:18	13
10:6,9-10,13	109
16:25-27	11,13
1 Corinthians	
1:10	69
2:7-13	13
2:14	17,42,45,48,73,77,80
2:15-16	73
2:16	37,45,48,80
4:4,7	45
6:11	109
6:19-20	26
13:12	116
13:13	44
14:6	13
14:12	29

verse	page #
1 Corinthians	
15:9-10	48,105,112
15:10	30
15:21-22,40, 42-44,47-50	76
15:42-44	116
15:42-49	50
15:49	61
15:51	115
15:52-54,57	117
2 Corinthians	
3:18	61
4:3-4	17,42,77
4:6-7	91
4:13	110
5:17	37,43,66,67, 102,103
6:1-2	85
Galatians	
1:12	44
1:15-16	14
1:16	15
1:26-27	20
2:16	111
2:20	20,42,48,66, 70,102
3:23	14
5:16,18,22-25	109
5:22	111
Ephesians	
1:19	48

Scripture References (cont'd)

On Being Born Again

Jesus answered and said unto him, Verily, verily, I say unto thee,
Except a man be born again, he cannot see the kingdom of God.
Nicodemus saith unto him, How can a man be born when he is old?
Can he enter the second time into his mother's womb, and be born?
Jesus answered, Verily, verily, I say unto thee, Except a man
be born of water and of the Spirit, he cannot enter into
the kingdom of God. That which is born of the flesh is flesh;
and that which is born of the Spirit is spirit.
Marvel not that I said unto thee, Ye must be born again.
John 3:3-7

God's Way of His Salvation

Our Lord Jesus Christ made some very definitive statements about *becoming* a Saint (Christian) and *receiving* Eternal Life. Read the text verses (and John 1:11-12; 14:6 and Ephesians 2:8-9 below) carefully, and my further comments, and then if you need more explanation or answers to some questions please contact me or someone you know who can give you God's wisdom and answers:

> Jesus saith unto him, I am the way, the truth, and the life:
> no man cometh unto the Father, but by Me. John 14:6

> He came unto His own, and His own received Him not.
> But as many as received Him, to them gave He power to
> become the sons of God, even to them that believe on His
> name. John 1:11-12

> For by grace are ye saved through faith; and that not of
> yourselves: it is the gift of God: Not of works, lest any man
> should boast. Ephesians 2:8-9

Within these four passages is *God's Way of His salvation* from our being a sinner. Many other scriptures show *God's Way* to *Eternal Life* (Jesus) also. God tells us of our need for His salvation; that everyone will die the physical death, and then face the judgment of God. Some people call this salvation being *saved*. There is Truth in that, but I like to make it clear and complete that a *New Spiritual Birth* more definitely describes *becoming* a Saint (Christian) and *knowing* you have become one.

127

So, let me share Truth shown four ways in the verses above: *God's salvation* is...

- only through the Lord Jesus Christ (by His Grace) and His blood shed on His Cross.
- only through a new Supernatural Spiritual Birth...a Holy Spirit accomplished Spiritual Birth (this is being *Born Again*).
- only as a gift of God. A gift cannot be earned, cannot be worked for, cannot be achieved by any of our efforts...just *received*.
- it is a must...no way around it. Jesus pronounced it. Jesus provided for it.

This is the New Birth (being Born Again). This New Birth is *God's Way* of salvation. Think about this: *birth brings life*. The Spiritual Birth brings forth the Spiritual Life. Saints have it now, and it continues with God after the physical life is over. That is Eternal Life.

Now, here is mankind's basic dilemma...anyone who has not been *Supernaturally Spiritually Born Again* thinks the way to Heaven is a path of *good works*. However, God's standard is perfection. Jesus Himself was perfect. And God says:

> But as He which hath called you is holy, so be ye holy in all manner of conversation (behavior); Because it is written, Be ye holy; for I am holy. 1 Peter 1:15-16

Are you perfect? Are you holy? Does a sinner live up to that? Does a Saint live up to that? Well, we all know the Truth is that a sinner living a perfect life is impossible. But God sent His perfect Son to be the perfect substitutionary, all-sufficient atoning sacrifice for all sinners' sin at His Cross of Calvary. And to give us the opportunity to BE Holy in God's Eyes. You may not understand that, but it is God's Truth.

Full forgiveness of one's sin can only come through a sinner confessing their sin, asking God for His forgiveness, receiving His Grace (His payment) by trusting in the Lord Jesus Christ and His death and shedding of His blood for that perfect sacrifice for one's sin. Then the new Saint is *perfect*. Being made *Holy* in God's eyes. That is known as *receiving Christ*. The Greek for *receive/receiving* in this manner is *lambano*. To take, to get hold of, to own.

The *perfection* in a Saint is Holy Spirit and His Soul. A Saint with Holy Spirit functioning out of Holy Soul will yield *perfection*.

Now good works do matter for a Saint (Christian), but only after salvation, not to escape God's righteous judgment. Even after salvation, any good Spiritual works are of God through a Saint, His Grace.

> For we are His workmanship, created in Christ Jesus
> unto good works, which God hath before ordained
> that we should walk in them. Ephesians 2:10

Is there a *perfect* prayer to pray for God's forgiveness and gift of *Eternal Life?* Perhaps. But God knows a repentant heart and a sinner's desire for *trusting Christ* for His salvation and His forgiveness. The following will help you with a *righteous prayer* if that is your desire:

> *Dear Lord Jesus Christ, I thank You for dying upon Your Cross for me, a guilty sinner, shedding Your blood to pay the penalty for my sin. I ask You, Lord Jesus, to have mercy on me. I believe You are the Way, the Truth, and the Life. And there is no other. I desire to be Supernaturally Spiritually Born Again. I deny and cease from any self-effort to save myself. I can't save myself. I call on Your mercy. I trust Your payment for my sin, and accept, and receive You gladly, as my Savior.*
>
> *Thank You for cleansing me and forgiving me of all my sin – past, present, and future. I believe, and by Your Holy Spirit now Living in me, KNOW I am redeemed, and You will never leave me nor forsake me. You are Lord Jesus Christ my Savior, my Lord, my God, my Life – forever! Amen.*

Just as you are *Born Again* by God's Grace when you trust in the Lord Jesus Christ and His payment, you are kept by God's Grace for all Eternity. Enjoy God's Mercy, His Love, His Grace NOW and for all Eternity as a *Born Again* child of God, one who once WAS a sinner but is NOW a HOLY Saint (Christian).

On Being Spirit-filled

And be not drunk with wine, wherein is excess;
but be filled with the Spirit.
Ephesians 5:18

God's Way of Be-being Filled

I remember being shown and told about Christians needing to be Spirit-filled soon after being Born Again in 1980. But I also remember asking two questions: why? or how? I never got a good answer.

The answers varied from *because God says so* to *you know,* to *you just get filled,* to *it is something God does for us,* or *it is how we are to live the Christian life.* So, I went on my merry way. Never getting any more, always searching for a clearer, more complete description of *being Spirit-filled.* And HOW to *be filled with Holy Spirit.* In fact, I later learned that the Greek means to *be being Spirit-filled.* A 24/7/52 filling.

Oh, I also remember being told that I should beware of *getting too much of the Spirit.* That was a no-no in the circles I was in. You know, the Charismatics and Assemblies were *out-on-a-limb* with this, and I needed to avoid that. So, here again I went on searching in my merry way.

In fact, in my first pastorate I had a sweet older lady who would come up to me at the back door of the sanctuary on a Sunday where I had mentioned Holy Spirit more than once, and she would tell me, "You are getting Him, Pastor!" Well, I knew who she watched on TV and sent money to. I did not put much merit in her exaltation.

But, one day as I was focusing on Galatians Chapter 5, *walking in the flesh* vs *walking in the Spirit,* God started bringing me His Truth that led to me having the proper knowledge of this whole thing. So, let me see if I can give someone who has the same, or similar, questions some clarity…

- to be *filled with Holy Spirit* is to *be being filled* with the Life of the Lord Jesus Christ. The result? The manifestation of Christ's Life in our earthsuit through Christ's Spirit and Christ's Soul in us.
- the *how* is simply to *abandon* OUR strength and flesh to Holy Spirit, *ask* Him to fill us, *believe* and *trust* that He has. This is a *Spiritual* transaction that cannot be explained or understood in any other way. It is *His Way,* not man's way.

130

- the best reason *why* is because God has told us this is *His Way* of *Life as a Christian*. That encompasses all God tells us in the *New Testament, His Way* of the *New Covenant*.
- to *walk in the Spirit* is to *walk in dependence on the Spirit*. Our weakness leads to dependence. Our strength (a characteristic of pride and flesh) leads to independence.

If a *Saint* (every Christian is a *Saint*) is at any time NOT *filled with Holy Spirit* that means his earthsuit (the housing of our Spirit and 2 souls) is *abandoned* in some part to his *flesh* (the control of his *carnal soul*). Out of *that heart* will flow something in animosity to God.

Now here is something that is not on this subject explicitly, but can be of help: God tells us in *2nd Corinthians 5:16-17*:

Wherefore henceforth know we no man after the flesh: yea, though we have known Christ after the flesh, yet now henceforth know we him no more. Therefore if any man be in Christ, he is a new creature: old things are passed away; behold, all things are become new.

Did you get that? Spiritually, we are to *know no man after the flesh* (the earthsuit). What else is there? *Know all men after their spirit.* HOW? By our new Creation in the Holy Spirit of God. Separate the physical from the spiritual. Know every person whether they are a new Creation, Born Again, or not. As far as knowing Christians, we must know also *which soul* they are *living* out of at any moment.

The *Good News* is that *being Spirit-filled* is not a complicated or difficult challenge. It is quite the opposite. *God's Way* is always the *easy Way* for us. God does all the work! We just have to do one thing: Believe, Trust, and Receive: BE BEING SPIRIT-FILLED! 24/7/52.

131

Recognizing the Source of LIFE
Of the Spirit-filled Saint

Visible Actions	"unshakeable faith" "unwavering faith" We abandon to God Our words and actions We are strengthened We have courage, we risk We want to do We go without knowing **BUT NONE OF THIS IS ME…IT IS CHRIST!**		
Visible Recognition	**WE SEE, HEAR, & KNOW GOD** w/our Spiritual Eyes, Spiritual Ears, & Spiritual Mind		
Invisible Controls	We believe God	We have confidence in God	We trust God
Invisible Recognition	We use our Spiritual Eyes, Spiritual Ears, & Spiritual Mind The Eyes, Ears, & Mind of Christ we were given at our New Birth		
Invisible Cause SOURCE of LIFE	Salvation - Indwelling of Holy Spirit God confirms our believing, confidence, & trust with the gifts of **HIS FAITH & HIS GRACE**		
Invisible Rule	**God Speaks**		
Invisible Goal	We want to: **See God - Hear God - Know God**		

About the Author

Since September of 2015, the author has been living in seclusion and solitude with God in a relatively secluded country setting, removed from the daily hysteria of ordinary life. During this time, what God had poured into the past 43 years is now in writing. By reading B. Lee McDowell's works, you can experience the most uncomplicated, completely enunciated, and direly needed Truths that all Saints should know.

Born into a family of educators, B. Lee McDowell instead set his sights on other fields and first became a professional golfer before settling into a lucrative sales career. But God had different plans.

With a father who was a college tennis player and later a multi-sport coach, Lee was involved in athletics from an early age. An injury at age 12 re-directed his athletic plans, and he turned to golf, playing on the Texas A&M University Golf Team, ultimately winning the Texas State Amateur Golf Championship, and playing on the PGA Tour for a couple of years.

In his late twenties, he became a salesman, where he worked his way up to become a manager/vice-president of the world's largest small boat dealership, Louis DelHomme Marine in Houston, Texas.

But in 1981, God called Lee to a life of ministry. He studied at Southwestern Baptist Theological Seminary, and began his life's calling. Having been a minister in various forms in various towns for 43 years, his extensive experiences and acquaintances have given him a broad perspective of *Life as a Christian* showing in his writings.

Life changed in 2003 when Lee suffered a major heart attack. God then had him serving in part-time pastoral roles until his 70th birthday. At that point, God moved Lee into writing books and blogs, and doing discipleship training and counseling. From an encounter at a men's retreat with Greg Wray, a Saint from California, he got the idea of doing ministry at a local park on Sunday mornings. Lee led the ministry, *Christ in the Park*, at Festival Park in Nacogdoches for 5 years. With his wife, Barbara, and friends, Rick and Abby West. Then he had *Christ at the Market,* on Saturday mornings at the Nacogdoches Farmer's Market with David & Diane Ruby (Ruby Farm). Today, he is writing, teaching, and speaking as God leads.

B. Lee McDowell is the president of Lee McDowell Christian Ministries, a preaching, teaching, discipleship-making ministry. Lee and his wife of 56 years, Barbara, have 2 children and four grandchildren.

BOOKS by B. Lee McDowell
Dowadad Press, Publisher
A division of Lee McDowell Christian Ministries, Inc.
www.blmcm.net
www.amazon.com/-/e/B083LQXJZ4

Books in Print

Seagulls Don't Lie!
The Truth will MAKE you free!

God's Words Bring *Life*
Christ's Life becoming your Life

all i want is Jesus!
His Love, His Grace, His Sound Mind, His Shepherding

The Images of God & Man
17 diagrams explaining "spirit, soul, & body"

Study Guide – The Images of God & Man
Questions & discussions for The Images of God & Man

Putting the Handcuffs on God
False beliefs & actions stifle God's Power

The Math of Life
Experiencing the Life of Christ in your personal finances

The Parable of the Two Souls
Examining the two spiritual souls of Saints

Books to Come

The Pane of Christianity
A look at two sides to one Truth

Christ's Life as My Life
    A Daily Devotional giving Truth about Christ's Supernatural
    Spiritual Life Lived through His Saints

The Overlooked Fundamentals of Christianity
    Growing in God's Grace – MUCH more than "unmerited favor"
    Definitions, Diagrams, and Foundational Truths

all i want is Jesus! – Vol. 2
    His Presence, His Acceptance, His Faith, His Peace, His Joy, His
    Hope, His Mercy

Putting the Handcuffs on God – Vol. 2
    More false beliefs and actions stifling God's Power

Made in the USA
Monee, IL
05 October 2023